The Neighborhood by the Falls

Longfellow School
Decoration Day parade,
c. 1923

The Neighborhood by the Falls

A Look Back at Life in
LONGFELLOW

ERIC HART

LONGFELLOW HISTORY PROJECT

Minneapolis ❦ Longfellow Community Council ❦ 2009

© 2009 by Longfellow Community Council
All rights reserved.

2727 26th Avenue South
Minneapolis, MN 55406
612.722.4529
www.longfellow.org
admin@longfellow.org

Library of Congress Control Number: 2009925864
Printed in the United States of America

10 9 8 7 6 5 4 3 2 1

Sappi Fine Paper North America, Flo Dull Cover and Text
10% Post Consumer Waste

Editing: E. B. Green Editorial, St. Paul
Indexing: Ken Green
Design: Bill Lundborg/West 44th Street Graphics

On the cover: Minnehaha Falls and rustic bridge, c. 1908

CONTENTS

Preface — vi

Introduction — viii

1. Mighty Mississippi — 1

2. Early Settlement — 17

3. Longfellow in 1900 — 29

4. Social Life — 43

5. Entertainment — 61

6. Building Longfellow — 77

7. 21st Century — 101

   References — 115

   Illustration Credits — 121

   Index — 122

PREFACE

For five years the all-volunteer Longfellow History Project (LHP), operating under the auspices of the Longfellow Community Council (LCC), has worked to interpret and disseminate the history of Longfellow. Its aim has been to make neighborhood history more visible and widely known by sponsoring walking tours of historic areas, collecting oral history interviews of residents, and producing this history of the neighborhood.

The stories and topics presented here tell the larger story of how the Longfellow neighborhood came to be and of the people in it. We explore facets of neighborhood history illustrating the forces and people who created the area we enjoy today. Given the large geographical area and multitude of stories, we focus mostly on the formative decades before 1930, the forces shaping the neighborhood, and what everyday life was like.

Much of the research and writing first appeared in the neighborhood history-tour guidebooks. LHP organized and led three tours; for each of them, volunteers Iric Nathanson, Kathy Swenson, and Eric Hart produced a 25-page guidebook providing details on each of the tour stops. In September 2005, the first walking tour visited historic sites of the 27th Avenue* and Lake Street area. In May 2006, the second walking tour covered West River Parkway sites from 36th to 44th Streets. In July 2008, LHP organized a third tour, this one by bicycle, focusing on the industrial areas and other historic sites at the western edge of the neighborhood. The Neighborhood by the Falls builds on those guidebooks, supplementing that material with topics compiled by the LHP over eight-plus years.

Eric Hart, chair of the LHP, was the content editor and lead writer/researcher for the book. He conceived its outline and chapter structure, collected previously written pieces, did additional research as needed, solicited research and writing help from other LHP members, called and chaired meetings, and pulled it all together. He was also the primary contact for the editor and graphic designers hired to produce the book.

The book was nevertheless the work of many, spearheaded by the LHP but enriched by contributions from other residents, as well as from the staffs of several libraries.

The LHP spent countless hours researching, writing, meeting, and deciding. Individual members brought their passions and skills to various aspects of the project: Joan Krey did biographical and background research for chapters 1–6, found reference materials, and reviewed manuscript drafts. Iric Nathanson wrote the funding proposal, did research for chapter 6, and handled production of the history-tour guidebooks. Ryan North did research and writing for chapter 7. Kathy Swenson did research and writing for chapter 1 (Mississippi River), chapter 2 (Indian and natural history), chapter 5 (movie theaters), and chapter 6 (schools), reviewed drafts, found and scanned illustrations, and provided guidebook research and writing.

The following individuals and groups provided valuable and hard-to-find information and illustrations. Carolyn Carr did research and writing for chapter 1 (river gorge restoration). John DeWitt did streetcar and railroad research. Julianne Haahr found chapter 4 illustrations and reviewed drafts. Hillary Oppmann did research and writing for chapter 7 (rain gardens).

Barbara Williams, of Drexel University College of Medicine, Archives and Special Collections on Women in Medicine and Homeopathy, found source material and illustrations on the Wass sisters, as did the Northwestern University Archives. The Harness Racing Museum and Hall of Fame, Goshen, New York, provided source material and illustrations on Minnehaha Driving Park. Thanks to the Mississippi National River and Recreation Area, National Park Service, for help with illustrations for chapters 1, 2 and 7. Loren Williams provided the Riverview Theater photos.

*A note on the text: All avenues mentioned are south (as 28th Avenue South) and all streets are east (as 42nd Street East) to avoid repetition. The punctuation of some historical quotes has been modernized for clarity.

Many thanks to the Longfellow Community Council and its Neighborhood Revitalization Program for the grant that made publication of this book possible, and to Executive Directors Katie Hatt and Melanie Majors for their encouragement and support.

— The Longfellow History Project Committee

Eric Hart, Chair
Joan Krey
Iric Nathanson
Ryan North
Kathy Swenson

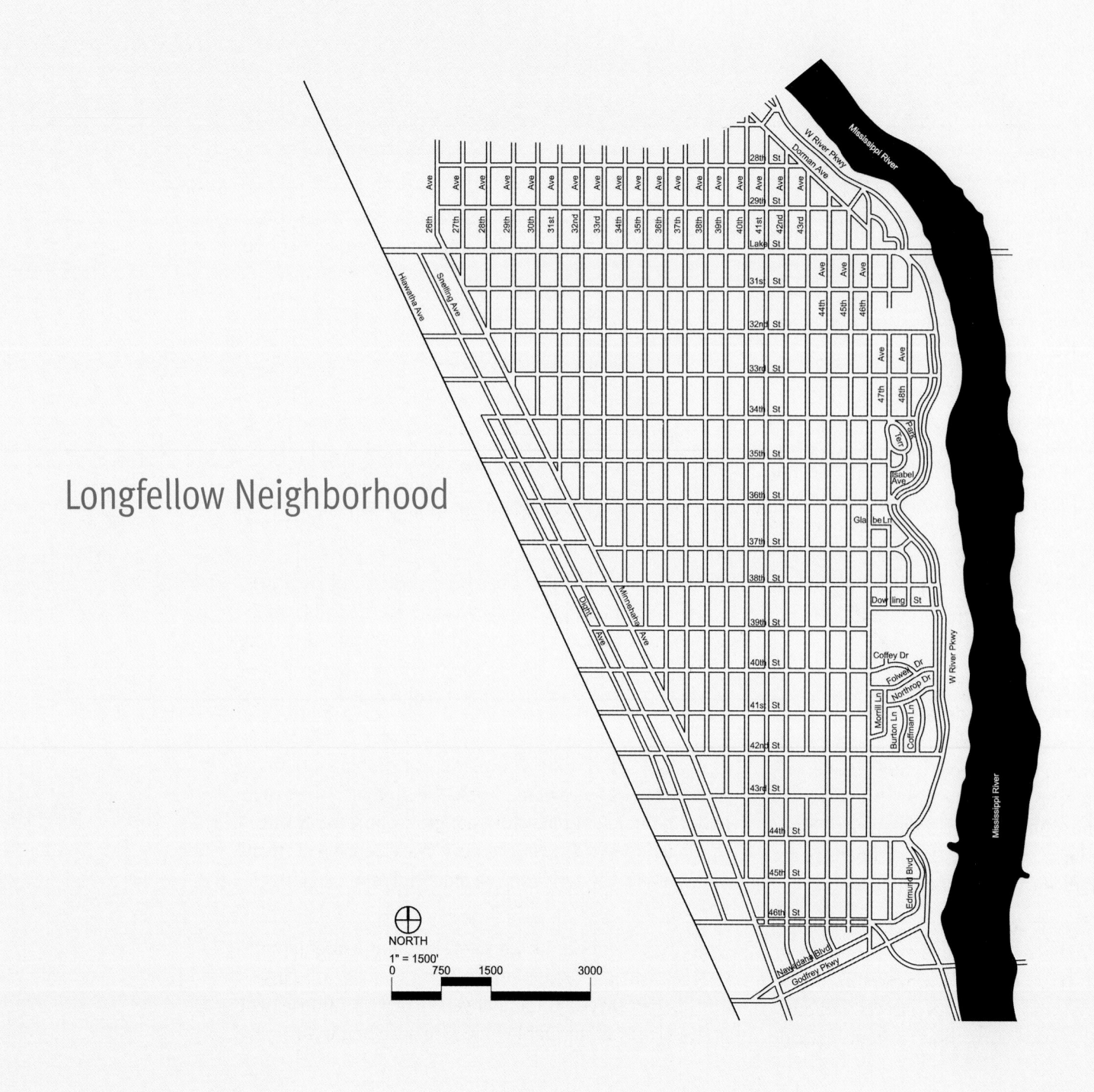

Longfellow Neighborhood

INTRODUCTION

The Falls of St. Anthony on the Mississippi River—and the geology that made both possible—in turn made possible the major city that Minneapolis is today. Waterpower produced by the falls energized the flour-milling and lumber industries developing in the city. As a result, Minneapolis became a major center of commerce in the Upper Midwest, and the growing city eventually reached the Longfellow area, filling it with modest homes and a scattering of industry along its western edge.

The Longfellow community has always been a little out of the way, tucked into the city's southeast corner and wedged between Hiawatha Avenue and the Mississippi. The Midtown Greenway along the 27th Street rail corridor forms its northern boundary. Minnehaha Park sits at its southern tip. At the edge of the city and at a distance from the congestion of downtown Minneapolis and the prestige of the Chain of Lakes, Longfellow became home to working-class people who built modest bungalows.

Longfellow gets its name from the 19th-century poet Henry Wadsworth Longfellow. In 1855, Longfellow penned *Song of Hiawatha*, an epic poem loosely based on Dakota and Ojibwe legends. The poem chronicles the story of the warrior Hiawatha, who in his journeys falls in love with the maiden Minnehaha, who lives by Minnehaha Falls. Neither Minnehaha nor Hiawatha are the names of historical persons, but their inclusion in Longfellow's poem forever associates them with this part of Minnesota.

Minnehaha was the first of Longfellow's names to show up on maps, shortly after the poem was published. Then, in the late 1800s and early 1900s, the names Hiawatha, Nokomis, and Nawadaha showed up on streets and business around south Minneapolis. In 1891 the republished poem—with Frederic Remington illustrations—sparked renewed interest in the work. Schoolchildren studied his poems and celebrated his birthday.

The name Longfellow is relatively new to the neighborhood. Historically, the area was part of the 12th Ward but without a real identity of its own. Smaller sections of the area, like Seven Oaks and the Hiawatha district, had names that didn't stick. In the 1930s, south Minneapolis, including Longfellow, was known as Southtown.

Longfellow is the name of the first modern school in the neighborhood, and it was the nomer of a smaller neighborhood when the city first defined neighborhoods in the 1950s. The Minneapolis Planning Department in the mid-1970s lumped the Seward neighborhood with what is now Longfellow into one large planning district.

The Longfellow of today dates from 1983, when neighborhood residents decided to split from Seward and form the Longfellow Community Council. The council represents four neighborhoods—Longfellow, Cooper, Howe, and Hiawatha—delimited by 1950s elementary-school boundaries.

Compared with other parts of Minneapolis, Longfellow is a young neighborhood. Residential development patterns were such that areas of the city to the north and west were built up first; Longfellow did not grow appreciably until the first decade of the 20th century. The extension of streetcar lines into the area was the main driver of residential development.

As a consequence of its later development, Longfellow was home to a number of institutions such as orphanages and large-scale entertainment venues such as amusement parks. Open and available land also attracted industry to the northwest corner of the neighborhood in the 1870s, laying the groundwork for a century of implement manufacturing near the intersection of Minnehaha Avenue and Lake Street.

The same can be said for grain elevators and mills, which first appeared in the 1880s along the railroad tracks and Hiawatha Avenue. Finally, from about 1885 to 1905, small-scale dairy farms filled the unused land as landowners waited for development to reach the area.

Despite its late residential development, the Longfellow area was part of Minnesota's early white settlement. In the 1820s, when Fort Snelling was the only appreciable white settlement in what would be the state of Minnesota, soldiers traveled the path of today's Minnehaha Avenue on the way to their mills at the Falls of St. Anthony.

In the 1800s many passed through the area, but few called it home. By the 1850s, the land opened to settlement, and New Englanders staked farmstead claims there. Native American and settler interaction was common in the 1850s but ended in 1862 as a result of the Dakota War. Minnehaha Falls was a popular tourist attraction through the second half of the 19th century, bringing many people through the neighborhood on railroad and streetcar lines.

The Mississippi River, while hidden nearly a hundred feet below street level in a gorge, is a powerful force in Longfellow. Potential waterpower and steamboat navigation attracted the first white settlers in the 1850s, but the swift, rocky river proved too much of an obstacle to these soon abandoned ambitions. More than a thousand feet wide, the gorge, a formidable obstacle to crossing, spawned the creation of three distinctive bridges over the river.

Like Minneapolis as a whole, Longfellow experienced population and job losses after World War II. Larger-scale redevelopment projects started in the 1970s and continued until the early 1990s—mostly in the vicinity of the Lake Street and Minnehaha Avenue intersection. Revitalization efforts increased in the late 1990s, focusing on home and historic commercial building renovation. Interest in the neighborhood and revitalization efforts have continued into the 21st century, raising home prices to unprecedented levels.

Major infrastructure projects completed in the first years of the new century include the rebuilding of Lake Street and the construction of the Midtown Greenway. New condominium and apartment complexes have started up on underutilized industrial parcels. The new century's real-estate boom has gone bust, but the neighborhood, with solid housing stock and desirable location, is positioned to weather the storm.

1/Mighty Mississippi

Mighty Mississippi

The Mississippi, arguably America's greatest river, runs dramatically along and forms the eastern boundary of the neighborhood. The scenic river gorge guides the river on its journey south, hiding it from view and disturbance by urban life.

Overleaf—
Looking north from the Lake Street Bridge, c. 1905. The Short Line Bridge is at top left. Meeker Island lies just beyond the right pier.

The Longfellow neighborhood's predevelopment landscape embodied several ecosystems, from prairie to dense forest. Along Minnehaha Avenue and six to ten blocks to the east, prairie reigned. Within six blocks of the Mississippi River, the scenery changed to that of oak savanna—scattered oak trees on prairie. Finally, from the top of the river bluff to the river's edge, was a dense forest with many types of hardwood trees and an understory of bushes such as hazelnut. Within this forest were different forest ecosystems, most notably the maple-basswood forest at the southern end of the neighborhood. The prairie, having succumbed to the plow and later to residential development, is gone now. But most of the scattered oaks have survived; the river bluff and gorge still support a dense hardwood forest.

The Mississippi, arguably America's greatest river, runs dramatically along and forms the eastern boundary of the neighborhood. The scenic river gorge guides the river on its journey south, hiding it from view and disturbance by urban life.

Minneapolis would not have become a great city and the milling capital of the world without the Mississippi River and its geology, prone to the formation of waterfalls. But recession of the Falls of St. Anthony several thousand years before had left the riverbed strewn with slabs of limestone and numerous rapids, islands, and sandbars. Steamboats, even with their shallow hulls, dared not steam to the falls except during times of high water. This and hard economic times thwarted the early efforts of land speculators and traders to create a new town, "Falls City," along the riverside.

As railroads began to dominate transportation after the Civil War, interest in the river for navigation waned. For the rest of the 19th century, the Mississippi was mostly a place to float logs to sawmills and dispose of waste. Various channel improvement projects, undertaken to break the railroad monopoly during the late 1800s, failed to entice commercial traffic back to the river. Not until the first decade of the 20th century were more serious attempts made to improve navigation through the use of locks and dams. Even these improvements failed to make much difference in commercial traffic.

The Mississippi before white settlement in the area looked much different from the way it appears today. Four large islands and several smaller ones dotted the river as late as 1899 between the what are now the Short Line rail bridge and Minnehaha Park. In many places, the river did not take up the entire channel (see page 1). Not until 1917, when Lock and Dam No. 1 was completed, did the river take on its current width and lakelike appearance.

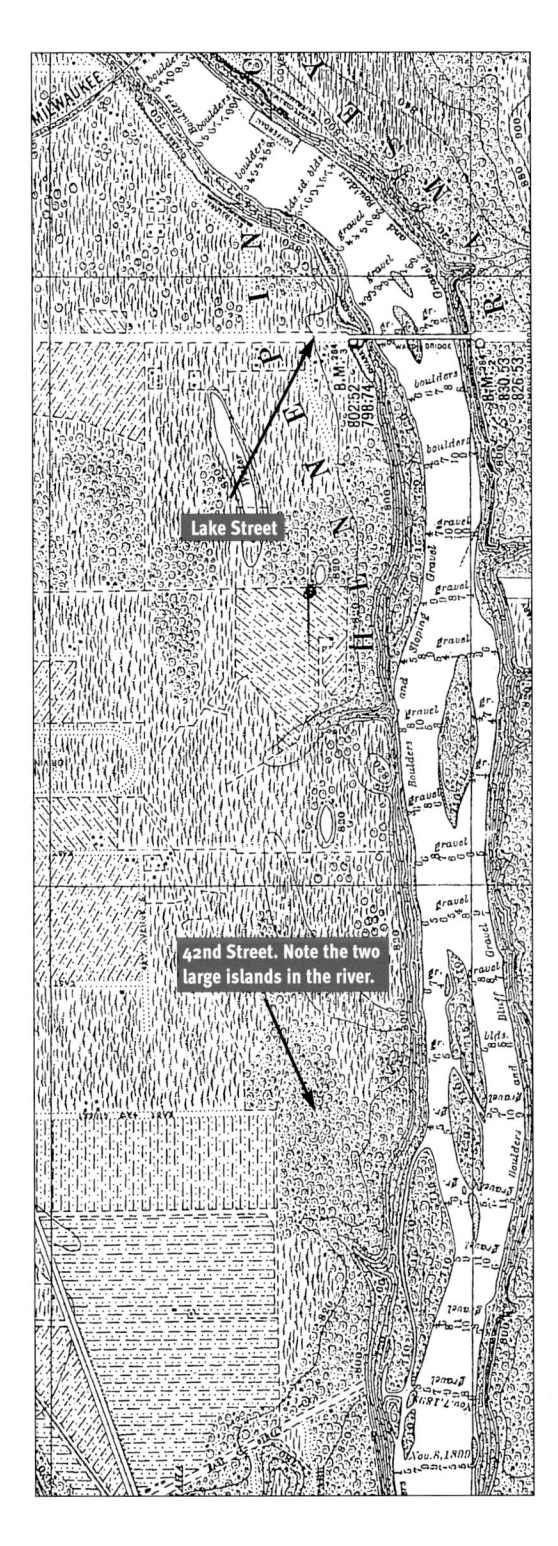

As the neighborhood developed, an increasing amount of untreated waste and sewage flowed into the river at 38th Street and other places. The construction of Lock and Dam No. 1 exacerbated the pollution problem, trapping pollutants behind the dam and creating a dead zone, devoid of fish. By the 1930s, enough political will existed in Minneapolis and St. Paul to build a joint sewage-treatment plant on Pig's Eye Island in St. Paul. The Mississippi quickly recovered. Not as clean today as it could be, the river nevertheless is much less polluted than it was in the early 1900s.

The last several decades have seen renewed interest in the ecology of the river gorge and in preserving and restoring the remnant ecosystems that have survived 150 years of disturbance and development. In recognition of the river's significance, Congress designated the 72 miles of Mississippi River corridor running from Ramsey and Dayton on the north through the Twin Cities to just below Hastings a national park in 1988. Since then, local groups like the Longfellow Community Council and the Minneapolis Park and Recreation Board have undertaken many projects to restore and preserve the ecosystems and natural areas of the gorge. These community-based efforts continue to improve the gorge while engaging local residents in stewardship.

◂ Mississippi River from the Short Line Bridge to Minnehaha Park, 1899. Note the island straddled by the Lake Street Bridge and the big islands in the vicinity of 36th and 42nd Streets.

Native Vegetation

A stroll through the Longfellow neighborhood is a walk through an urban forest. Trees line every street, forming a "leafy river" that complements the Mississippi. Yards bloom with native plants though "wildlife" is typically limited to squirrels. Much has changed over the past century and a half, yet some parts of the native landscape persist.

The native people of the area left no record describing the landscape before white settlers arrived. Explorers and settlers, however, provided many written descriptions. Henry Lewis wrote in 1848:

> From the Falls of St. Anthony an enormous prairie reaches out in all directions. Toward the north and the west it disappears on the distant horizon; toward the southwest it touches upon the St. Peter's [Minnesota] River and stretches for another eight miles over the bottom lands formed by the junction of the same with the Mississippi . . . toward the south it reaches as far as Fort Snelling, which is built on the high promontory overlooking the confluence of the two rivers. There is in this region much of interest for the naturalist, as well as for the admirer of the scenic beauty, especially among the thrilling waterfalls; one of these, about two and one-half miles distant from Fort Snelling, is called "Brown's Fall"— "Little Fall"—or also "Calhoun's Fall"—and is of all of them by far the most interesting.

John Stevens elaborated:

> Toward Minnehaha the prairies were two or three miles long and extended to Lake Calhoun and Harriet . . . the way to Fort Snelling was a lone oak tree about half way to Little Falls Creek. It was a species of poplar and had escaped the prairie fires . . . This was the only landmark then on the prairie between Minnehaha Falls and the west bank of the Falls of St. Anthony. It was far from being a pretty tree, but it served an excellent purpose during the winter months when the Indian trail was covered with snow, as a guide to the few travelers who passed over the lonely prairie.

Regular prairie fires controlled woody plants on the prairie and invigorated the soil. Mrs. C. A. Smith remembered: "The prairies bloomed with wildflowers, presenting a perfectly lovely sight. A fire in 1856 had resulted in great thickets of blackberries of huge size a couple of years later. In 1858 cranberries also grew in huge quantities in the swamps. Hazelnuts were so numerous that they could not all be picked."

The diversity of plants supported a variety of wildlife. Eli Pettijohn recalled shooting a buffalo in the area in 1841; in 1850 someone saw a seven-foot snake near Minnehaha Falls. Imagine flocks of birds so numerous that they blocked the sunlight in passing: "The pigeons were so plentiful in 1854 and flew so low that farm implements could be used to kill them. Countless pigeons migrated every spring. They could be seen in countless numbers on the old dead trees or 'slab trees.' "

Even as the settlers changed the landscape, remnants of the earlier landscape remained. The *East Lake Shopper*, published from the 1930s to the 1950s, recalled the neighborhood of the 1890s: "South of the railroad tracks [about 27th Street] there was only Minnesota prairie . . . Out in the Lake neighborhood, from 34th to 38th Avenues, was a swampy area affectionately known as the 'Frog Pond.' "

Indeed, the Mississippi that native peoples, explorers, and settlers saw was different from the waterway of today. Zebulon Pike described the river in 1805 as "almost one continued rapid, aggravated by the interruption of 12 small islands." Another explorer, George Featherstonhaugh, agreed, stating that only mosquitoes outnumbered the islands. Before the installation of locks and dams, the level of the river varied. Sometimes it was so high and

Fort Snelling, c. 1850, painting by Henry Lewis. This view to the northwest shows the prairie covering most of south Minneapolis to the right beyond the fort.

fast flowing that a continuous rapid filled the gorge, while at others the river was rather shallow and slow moving. The river and islands provided habitat for turtles, mussels, birds, a variety of mammals, and as many 120 varieties of fish.

Extending up the banks of the gorge was a rich diversity of plants. Stephen Long in 1817 was impressed by the landscape:

> The place where we encamped last night needed no embellishments to render it romantic in the highest degree. The banks on both sides of the river are about one hundred feet high, decorated with trees and shrubbery of various kinds. The post hickory, walnut, linden, star tree, white birch, and the American box; also various evergreens, such as the pine, cedar, juniper, etc., added their embellishments to the scene. Amongst the shrubbery were the prickly ash, plum, and cherry tree, the gooseberry, the black and red raspberry, the chokeberry, grapevine, etc. There were also various kinds of herbage and flowers, among which were the wild parsley, rue, spikenard, etc., red and white roses, morning glory, and various other handsome flowers.

Almost a century later, the bluffs still retained much of their original character. Victor Nelson, who grew up in the area in the early years of the 20th century, recalled the river and islands of his youth: "We used to pick wildflowers on the river bank and wild strawberries." Before the Ford Dam (Lock and Dam No. 1) was built, he remembered, "Our cows grazed all along the river bank. They would swim out to the islands in the river."

Mighty Mississippi ■ 5

While much of the neighborhood has changed, perhaps city leaders did heed some of Horace Cleveland's 1885 advice: "Preserve above all the wild and picturesque character of the river banks, and do not suffer them to be stripped of their foliage or scarred and seamed by excavation. The day is not distant when the thickly wooded banks, the deep and dark ravines, the rugged and precipitous rocks, and the picturesque cascades which form the shores of the majestic river will be regarded as your choicest possessions for the unique character they will confer upon the city."

Gorge Geology

In Longfellow, the Mississippi is nearly hidden in a gorge, the only true gorge along the entire stretch of the river. The gorge—75 to 100 feet deep and nearly 1,000 feet wide—offers spectacular vistas; its steep slopes have protected remnant native plant communities. In the exposed bluffs of the gorge are visible the sedimentary rocks formed from the ancient seas that covered the area 550 million years ago. The sand, silt, clay, and remnants of sea life in this ancient seabed compressed over time, forming the layers of St. Peter sandstone, Glenwood shale, and Platteville limestone we see today.

The gorge formed during relatively modern geologic times as a result of the last Ice Age. Advancing and retreating glaciers carved out valleys and deposited sediment while melting glacial ice created the rivers, forming the present-day landscape. The greatest of these rivers was River Warren, fed by Glacial Lake Agassiz. About 12,000 years ago, at the site of today's downtown St. Paul, River Warren became a thundering waterfall, 175 feet high and 2,700 feet across. It was roughly the size of the largest of today's Niagara Falls. The water pouring over the falls easily eroded the sandstone, setting the stage for the collapse of the shale and limestone layers.

Layers of bedrock showing the mechanism for the recession of the Falls of St. Anthony ▶

Sedimentary rock layers along the Mississippi River ▶

6 ■ The Neighborhood by the Falls

The erosion process caused the waterfall to recede up the river valley. About 10,000 years ago, at the junction of the Minnesota and Mississippi Rivers, the waterfall split. One falls went up the Minnesota River and ended about two miles upstream at Nine Mile Creek. The other, continuing up the Mississippi at an erosion rate of four or five feet per year, became known as the Falls of St. Anthony. The waterfall hit the area of the Longfellow community about 3,800 years ago. By the time settlement started in the 1850s, the falls had arrived at its current location near downtown Minneapolis. The U.S. Army Corps of Engineers (the Corps) installed a dike beneath the river and an apron over the falls between 1876 and 1884 to prevent further recession of the falls. Without these efforts, the geology of the area is such that the falls would have continued to recede, turning into a rapids near Nicollet Island.

A Wild and Rugged River

It's hard to imagine today, but 150 years ago the Mississippi between Minneapolis and St. Paul was strewn with large rocks. It was so shallow someone could walk across it without much trouble. As the Falls of St. Anthony receded, it left large chunks of limestone in its wake. This combined with the rapid drop of the riverbed to create countless rapids, sandbars, and other impediments to navigation. Islands were common—there were seven of some size between where the Short Line Bridge and Ford Bridge are today. Fishing was good, as the rocks and rapids created a varied habitat supporting 120 varieties (now only 30) of native fish.

Before the debut of the railroad (around the time of the Civil War) in Minnesota, settlers depended on steamboats to transport all goods and people into the territory. Much to the disappointment of early Minneapolitans, the river above Fort Snelling was all but unnavigable.

Occasionally a daring steamboat pilot made a run during very high water partway to the Falls of Anthony, but that was the exception. Making the river navigable proved a challenge fraught with political difficulties, a feat not fully accomplished until after World War II.

Falls of St. Anthony, 1857. While the river in Longfellow wasn't this rugged, this photo shows how the receding falls left huge chunks of limestone and a rough river in their wake.

Damming and Navigating the River

As early as 1852, river boosters planned projects to make the river navigable to the Falls of St. Anthony. Minnesota Territory was booming, and steamboats were the only economical way to haul goods and people to the frontier outpost. In 1857 a company was formed to build a lock and dam at Meeker Island, but despite several attempts, it failed. With the rise of railroads after the Civil War, river traffic dropped off dramatically except for that of the timber industry, which continued to float logs to the mills. Despite this lack of commerce, the Corps continued to plan for navigation improvement, hoping to return the river to the glory days of the 1850s. In 1873, Congress funded navigation improvements for the upper Mississippi, but disputes over a land grant delayed construction for more than 20 years.

Newton H. Winchell, 1900 ▶

Meeker Island Lock and Dam remnants, August 2, 2007. More than usual of the old lock was visible after the river was lowered 3½ feet to aid rescue efforts the day after the August 1, 2007, collapse of the I-35W bridge.

What's in a Name?

The Winchell Trail

Hidden along the steep bluffs of the river gorge is Winchell Trail, extending along the west bank of the Mississippi between Franklin Avenue and 44th Street. It follows the route of an old Indian trail connecting Minnehaha Falls with the Falls of St. Anthony.

Winchell Trail is the namesake of Newton Horace Winchell (1839–1914), a geologist who came to Minneapolis in 1872 to work for the University of Minnesota on the new Geological and Natural History Survey of Minnesota. Winchell traveled across the state, mapping its geologic resources. Locally, Winchell estimated the rate of recession of the Falls of St. Anthony between Fort Snelling and its current location. Winchell likely hiked the trail bearing his name, as geologic evidence of the recession of the falls is abundant in the river gorge. He impacted geologic research in determining the time of the last ice sheet's retreat from Minnesota. A glacial boulder with a plaque, near the west end of the Franklin Avenue Bridge, marks his contribution.

When Winchell died in 1914, a section of the old Indian path was named in honor of his many accomplishments. Improvements by the Works Progress Administration (WPA) in the late 1930s created many of the walls and steps that define the trail today. Those hiking the Winchell Trail today can see evidence of the area's past in the fossils in limestone, especially visible near 28th Street.

◀ Looking upstream (north) towards Meeker Island Lock and Dam, c. 1907. This is the Longfellow (west end) of the lock and dam. Note the bear-trap gates close to west shore.

Meeker Island Lock and Dam

By the early 1890s, the Corps had devised a plan to build two low dams with locks that would raise the level of the river sufficiently to open navigation to the Falls of St. Anthony. One dam was to be near Meeker Island (just south of the Short Line Bridge), the other (later known as Lock and Dam No. 1) near the mouth of Minnehaha Creek. Construction on Meeker Island Lock and Dam, the first on the entire Mississippi, started in 1898, with completion in 1907. Meeker was in operation just five years before the top five feet were demolished in 1912 to make navigation safe after Lock and Dam No. 1 opened to the south. The Meeker lock is still visible during low water on the St. Paul side, but the bear-trap gates on the Longfellow side that sent logs downriver have disappeared under the white-sand dredge spoils deposited there.

◀ Looking west from St. Paul towards Longfellow, c. 1904. The concrete wall and bollards at bottom are the same as the mostly submerged ones evident in the 2007 photo on page 8.

Mighty Mississippi ■ 9

What's in a Name?

Meeker Island

This island in the Mississippi is the namesake of Bradley B. Meeker (1813–1873), an early Minnesota judge. Meeker served in the first Minnesota Territorial Supreme Court from 1849 until 1853. After his brief judicial career, Meeker became a real-estate man. A staunch supporter of extending river navigation to Minneapolis, he purchased the ten-acre island near the east bank in the vicinity of today's 24th Street, in 1852. Three years later Minneapolis navigation proponents made the first proposal for a lock and dam on the island. The project stalled several times until the lock and dam finally were built half-a-mile downriver, just south of the Short Line Bridge. The pool created by Lock and Dam No. 1 partially submerged Meeker Island in about 1917; by the mid-1950s a casualty of post-World War II channel improvements, the island had completely disappeared.

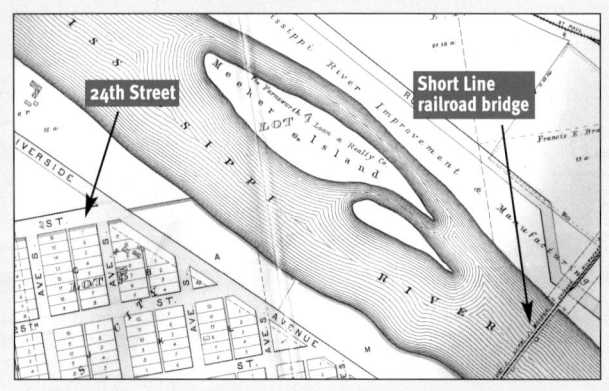

▶ Bradley B. Meeker, c. 1870

▶ Meeker Island, 1892

Lock and Dam No. 1

The Corps planned a second lock and low dam in the 1890s (along with the Meeker Island Lock and Dam) to raise water levels enough to make the river navigable to the Falls of St. Anthony. Just north of the mouth of Minnehaha Creek, it was started in 1903 and a good portion had been completed by 1907, when the Meeker Island Lock and Dam opened. In 1910, Congress approved a new strategy, abandoning low dams in favor of a single, higher lock that would support navigation and a dam to create hydroelectricity. Lock and Dam No. 1 was the location of choice.

When the new high dam opened in 1917, it supported navigation but provided no power. Congress had failed to fund a plant there, directing that some nonfederal entity develop the hydroelectric feature later. In 1920, Congress finally determined how nonfederal entities would operate hydroelectric dams, and local officials began the search for a potential user and developer. In the early 1920s, partially because of the prospect of cheap hydropower, the City of St. Paul was able to convince Ford Motor Company to open a new assembly plant by the lock and dam. Ford completed the hydroelectric plant in 1924 in time for the assembly plant's opening in 1925. The hydroelectric plant currently generates about 250,000 kilowatt-hours per day, about half going to the Ford plant, the balance being sold to Xcel Energy. The Corps added a second lock and dam in 1930.

10 ■ The Neighborhood by the Falls

◀ Looking upstream (north) towards Lock and Dam No. 1, c. 1925, before the appearance of the Ford Bridge and the hydroelectric plant

◀ Looking upstream (north) towards Lock and Dam No. 1 and the Ford Bridge, 1937. The powerhouse is at far right.

Mighty Mississippi ■ 11

Getting across the River

Short Line Railroad Bridge

After the Civil War, railroads became the favored mode of transportation; Minneapolis grew rapidly during the 1870s and 1880s. By the late 1870s the Short Line filled the need for a shorter rail connection between Minneapolis and St. Paul. The Chicago Milwaukee and St. Paul Railroad laid track for the Short Line across Longfellow in the vicinity of 27th Street. The Short Line Bridge across the Mississippi was completed in 1880. Fourteen stories high and 1,000 feet long, it was the first of three bridges across the Mississippi in the neighborhood. In 1901 it was widened and rebuilt to accommodate three tracks. It carried both freight and passenger trains such as the "Olympian." Passenger rail service ended in the 1970s, but several freight trains still use the bridge daily to access the grain elevators on Hiawatha Avenue.

Looking north at the Lake Street Bridge from the foot of Summit Avenue, St. Paul, c. 1890 ▶

Short Line Bridge with Chicago, Milwaukee and St. Paul "Olympian" passenger train heading west, c. 1912
▼

Lake Street–Marshall Avenue Bridge

In 1888 the first Lake Street Bridge was complete. The bridge connected Minneapolis and St. Paul, though in reality Lake Street was a rutted path and the cows outnumbered the people. At 1,271 feet long and 120 feet above the shallow river, the wrought-iron bridge was the second longest, open metal-arch bridge in the United States. Much of its construction took place during the brutally cold winter of 1887–88, as crews could work with relative ease on the frozen riverbed. The construction took on some elements of a circus act—installation required throwing thousands of red-hot metal rivets from the frozen riverbed to members of the crew on the bridge, who had to catch and drive them into place!

At first, the bridge serviced only pedestrian and wagon traffic. Then, in 1905, the Twin City Rapid Transit Company paid to have the bridge widened to accommodate the new Selby-Lake interurban streetcar line between Minneapolis and St. Paul. The bridge was in service for just over a century; in the years before the opening of the I-94 bridge, it was one of the busiest two-lane bridges in the United States.

12 ■ The Neighborhood by the Falls

The new Lake Street Bridge from the foot of Summit Avenue in St. Paul, 2007

The New Lake Street Bridge

By the time construction began on the new Lake Street Bridge in 1989, the old bridge had definitely seen better days. The speed limit on the bridge was 20 mph; pedestrians and motorists alike could see the Mississippi through holes in the bridge's deck. An inspection of the bridge in June 1987 showed serious problems. Consequently, several months later, Metro Transit buses were banned from the bridge, and smaller shuttle buses began taking passengers across the river.

Construction started on April 12, 1989, with a "water-breaking ceremony." Barely a year into the project, a part of the bridge under construction collapsed, killing an inspector. The old bridge remained in use until two lanes of the new one were complete. The new four-lane bridge, dedicated October 15, 1992, is wider and made of reinforced concrete.

Ford Bridge

The Ford Bridge, originally called the Intercity, arose between 1925 and 1927. It was the first modern bridge across the river in Longfellow. Built of cast concrete, it connected the booming bungalow neighborhood to the newly opened Ford plant on the St. Paul side of the river.

The East 25th Street streetcar line was extended from 46th Avenue across the bridge to the Ford plant in late 1927.

Aerial view, looking upstream (north) towards the Ford Bridge, c. 1927. Note the completed hydroelectric plant at Lock and Dam No. 1 at bottom right and the dam-caused pool upstream.

The Ford Bridge Drive-In, part of the drive-in restaurant craze of the 1950s, was on the northwest corner of 46th and 46th. This 1956 photo documents the beginning of its five-year run.

Mighty Mississippi ■ 13

Little commercial development occurred along 46th Street west of the bridge except for the corner of 46th Avenue and 46th Street, which sprouted gas stations on three of its four corners by the early 1930s. All but one closed by the end of World War II. A variety of businesses used the building on the northwest corner until 2006, when a condominium developer tore it down. The lot remains vacant.

Pollution Problems

The earliest European visitors to the upper Mississippi in the early 1800s found a pristine river with clear water, many rapids, and abundant fish. The river did not remain in this condition for long; as early as the 1850s, wood waste from the booming lumber mills near the Falls of St. Anthony was polluting the river. As the Twin Cities population grew through the last half of the 19th century, people and businesses dumped more and more waste into the river. The sanitary sewer system, expanded during the 1880s and 1890s, discharged ever-increasing amounts of untreated sewage directly into the Mississippi. Refuse and sewage from the Twin Cities was an impediment to navigation as far south as Lake Pepin.

The construction of the locks and dams was the breaking point, forcing city and state officials to address the pollution. Hoping waste would be swept downstream was no longer an option. The completion of Lock and Dam No. 1 in 1917 created a pool behind the dam into which flowed all but one of Minneapolis's sewers and 13 of St. Paul's, together containing about 65 million gallons of raw sewage daily. Within three years, some 3 million cubic yards of sludge accumulated behind the dam. By 1930, it was up to 12 feet deep.

White scum in front of 38th Street outlet, July 29, 1929 ▶

The Metropolitan Drainage Commission of Minneapolis and St. Paul formed in 1927 to examine the extent of river pollution and identify a plan for sewage treatment. It found that the Mississippi had become so polluted that touching or using it for any purpose was dangerous! A 1926 fish survey captured only two living fish in the 25-mile stretch downstream from the Falls of St. Anthony!

The pollution was at its worst in the Longfellow river-gorge segment. The commission in 1928 noted that at Lake Street, "Bubbles [of putrid gas] were continuously rising, and large masses of partly digested sludge were found floating at the surface. Dead fish were found floating in this ponded portion of the stream apparently having been overcome after entering the heavily polluted area from the less polluted region above the cities." Just above the dam was "a distinct sewage odor," while masses of gas-filled sludge, sleek, and scum covered the surface of the river.

After years of study and debate, Minneapolis and St. Paul finally broke ground on a joint sewage treatment plant in July 1934. The Pig's Eye treatment plant, the first on the Mississippi, opened in 1938. Within four months of the opening, the sludge mats had disappeared, and fish returned to the river gorge.

> ... individuals can make a difference. **Preventing leaves, litter, pet waste, and car fluids from entering the storm sewers is something** everyone can do to protect the Mississippi.

Today's river pollution problems aren't easily detected by sight or smell. Mercury from power plant emissions and phosphorous and nitrogen from fertilizers are modern problems. Extra phosphorous creates algae slime mats that consume oxygen and block sunlight vital to fish and plants. Nitrogen does not really affect the Mississippi River in Minnesota, but traveling downstream to the Gulf of Mexico, it contributes to the excess amounts creating the "Dead Zone," about 6,000 square miles devoid of plant and animal life.

Protecting the river may seem as daunting today as it was for the Metropolitan Drainage Commission. With the understanding that storm sewers drain directly to the river, however, individuals can make a difference. Preventing leaves, litter, pet waste, and car fluids from entering the storm sewers is something everyone can do to protect the Mississippi.

Recent River Gorge Restoration

The Mississippi River gorge has been dedicated parkland since 1903, when the Minneapolis Park Board bought and set it aside. Ten years later, the board carved out the first parkway along the river. But for most of the 20th century, little was done to protect or enhance the native vegetation remnants surviving in the gorge. From the mid-1990s, the Longfellow Community Council's River Gorge Committee has worked to preserve and enhance natural areas along the Mississippi in the Longfellow community. The committee identified the Longfellow portion of the gorge, between 27th Street and the Ford Bridge, for restoration, as it harbors remnant native plant communities including oak savanna, mesic prairie, floodplain forest, oak forest, and maple-basswood forest.

This overlook completed at 35th Street in 1999 is part of gorge restoration efforts.

Mighty Mississippi ■ 15

The remnant native prairie in the Mississippi gorge near 36th Street has benefited from intensive management since the mid-1990s. ▶

Seed collection from the native prairie in the gorge near 36th Street. The seed is used to restore oak savanna in the river gorge. ▶

As a first step, the River Gorge Committee in 1996 commissioned Close Landscape Architects to develop a concept plan. Out of this planning process came a strong recommendation from the community to preserve and enhance the Mississippi gorge as an ecological and environmental asset. Other identified goals included improving community ownership, access, and safety and enhancing public outdoor-recreation opportunities. The Longfellow Community Council (LCC) collaborated with the Minneapolis Park and Recreation Board as well as federal, state, and local agencies and several nonprofits to implement the plan. Between 1996 and 2006, the committee spent $338,500 in LCC Neighborhood Revitalization Program funds to leverage an additional $440,000 for projects in the gorge.

This funding has enabled improved access to trails along the river and the creation of a restoration plan to guide the continuing work. It has also provided incentive programs for neighborhood residents to make river-friendly improvements to their properties such as installing rainwater gardens and removing buckthorn (an invasive non-native shrub). In addition, it has supported River Gorge Stewards, a volunteer program engaging neighborhood residents in gorge restoration and maintenance activities since 2001.

2/Early Settlement

Early Settlement

For native peoples in the area, the Mississippi River provided food, water, and recreation, as well as a travel route between summer and winter camps and other sites. White settlers arrived in the early 1850s finding a landscape already influenced by soldiers at Fort Snelling decades earlier.

Overleaf and below—Indian tipis, site of Bridge Square (now downtown), Minneapolis, 1852. Native Americans and white settlers were in close contact during the 1850s. Settler John Stevens's home is barely visible next to the tipi at far right.

While the Dakota people left no trace of settlements in the Longfellow area, they had a strong influence on it. From establishing trails later used by white settlers to coming up with, or providing the inspiration for, many of the local place names, the Dakota made an impact. White settlement traces back to 1805, when Zebulon Pike acquired land for Fort Snelling and its nine-mile-square vicinity from the Dakota. The fort impacted the larger area when soldiers used Indian trails through the neighborhood to get to their mills at the Falls of St. Anthony. As soldiers went farther from the fort for firewood and food, they further changed the locale.

In 1851, the federal government's Traverse des Sioux treaty with the Dakota opened a floodgate of white settlers to a large part of Minnesota. Soon pressure mounted on the government to sell the remaining military reservation land, including all of the land that is now Longfellow. In anticipation of the sale, settlers rushed into the area in 1852 to claim nearly all the land. The land was surveyed in 1853, and in 1855 settlers could purchase the acres they had claimed.

The original settlers were of two groups—farmers and speculators. The land closest to Minnehaha Avenue was prairie suitable for farming and so claimed mostly by New England farmers. The speculators favored the land closest to the Mississippi River, which was less suitable for farming but for which they had plans for river commerce. A group of St. Anthony businessmen laid out a good-sized town, Falls City, north of present-day Lake Street, supposedly the new head of navigation on the Mississippi. These businessmen also planned to improve the Mississippi with a lock and dam and other improvements that would make the river more navigable. The Panic of 1857 and subsequent economic depression called a halt forever to their grandiose plans.

Indian and white settler interaction came to an abrupt end in 1862 after the Dakota War in southern Minnesota. After holding Dakota women, children, and old men in detention at Fort Snelling in the winter of 1862–63 and executing 38 hastily tried Dakota "warriors," the government deported the Dakota to reservations in South Dakota and Nebraska.

Native Americans in the Area

For native peoples in the area, the Mississippi River provided food, water, and recreation, as well as a travel route between summer and winter camps and other sites. The river served as a connection to a much larger native "neighborhood." West of the river stretched a great prairie useful for ceremonies, hunting, gardening, and travel.

The Dakota were a communal people to whom individual land ownership was a foreign concept. Their word for "earth"—*Unci Maka*—translates as "Grandmother Earth," indicating their view of the earth as an ancestor and elder. This placed them at great odds with white settlers.

Sites important to Native Americans line both the Mississippi and Minnesota Rivers. The Longfellow neighborhood lies between two of them—the Falls of St. Anthony and the confluence of the Mississippi and Minnesota Rivers. The Dakota had several names for the falls—*O-Wa-Mni* (whirlpool), *Ha-Ha Tanka* (big waterfall), and *Owahmenah* (falling water). They referred to the juncture of the Mississippi and Minnesota Rivers as *Mdote* (or *Bdote*, depending on the translation). Samuel Pond wrote in 1851 about Dakota beliefs: "One great natural fact which perhaps ought to be recognized and recorded at the start is this, vis: That the mouth of the Minnesota River . . . lies immediately over the centre of the earth and under the centre of the heavens."

Indian agent Lawrence Taliaferro drew a map showing native paths. One traces the route that Minnehaha Avenue follows today. Winchell Trail and West River Parkway follow another native path absent from that map.

After the Louisiana Purchase in 1803, President Thomas Jefferson sent Meriwether Lewis and William Clark to explore the Missouri River. He also sent Zebulon Pike up the Mississippi to obtain land for a future fort. In 1805 Pike negotiated the first treaty with native people in Minnesota at *Makoce Wakan*, where the Mississippi and Minnesota Rivers join. Today this site, in Fort Snelling State Park, is known as Pike Island.

Like the Indians, Pike recognized the power of the area. Built when rivers served as highways, the fort on the high river bluffs above the confluence offered a commanding view of river traffic and control of the waterways. The treaty established a military reservation roughly nine miles square. It stretched west to the Chain of Lakes,

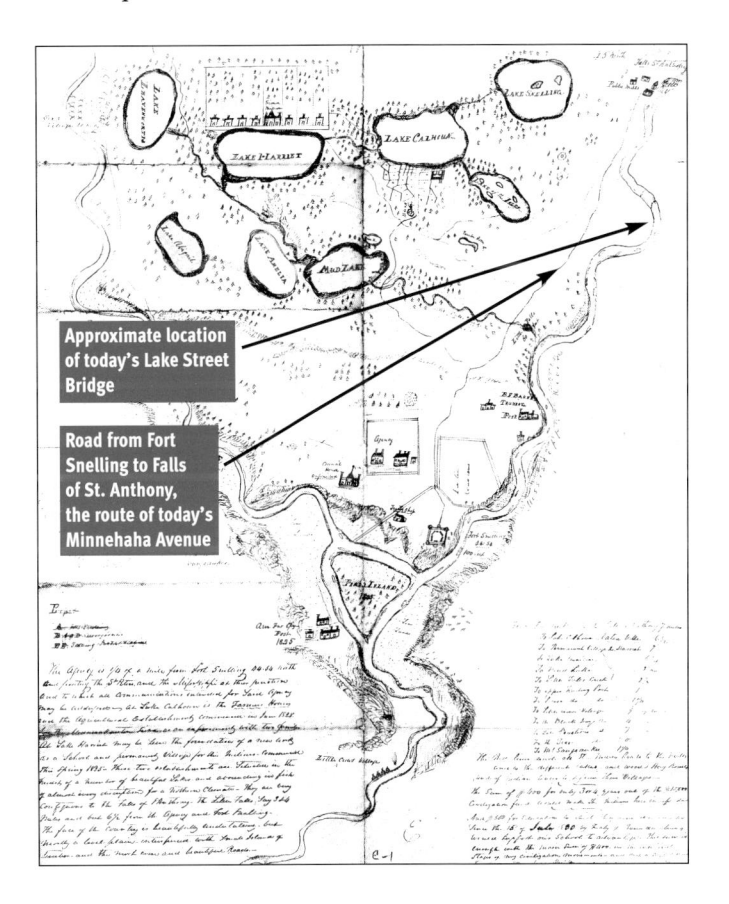

◀ *Map of Fort Snelling and Vicinity*, Lawrence Taliaferro, 1835, showing the road from Fort Snelling to Falls of St. Anthony and other native paths of that time

Captured Dakota people in fenced enclosure on Minnesota River below Fort Snelling, 1862–1863 ▶

north to Bassett's Creek, several miles south along the Minnesota River, and several miles east of Pike Island on the Mississippi. In modern terms, the reservation included nearly all of south Minneapolis north to Bassett's Creek (just north of downtown) and St. Paul north and east of Fort Snelling along the Mississippi.

The construction of Fort Snelling, begun in 1819, brought many changes to the area and to the Dakota. Soldiers began farming the prairie, grazing cattle, and building homes. Settlers squatted on the land, building homes and tilling the land. In the 1851 Traverse des Sioux treaty, the Dakota ceded all the land in Minnesota save for two small 150-mile strips along the Minnesota River. Fewer than 50 years after the signing of the first treaty on Pike Island in 1805, a way of life in Minnesota ended.

Despite the treaties, many Dakota at first remained in the area. John Stevens recalled in 1851 that two bands of Indians "encamped on the high land above the Falls for several weeks in July and August . . . They appeared again during the fall with large quantities of cranberries which the merchants and the citizens of St. Anthony were eager to purchase." The diminished reservation lands allotted to the Dakota offered little to hunt or gather, and when crooked agents and traders withheld treaty annuities and payments, the Dakota went hungry. Despite warehouses full of food near the reservations, officials ignored their pleas for food. In response, some hungry young warriors killed a farm family, igniting the Dakota War of 1862 (also known as the Great Sioux Uprising or Dakota Conflict) in southern Minnesota.

Ultimately, U.S. and Minnesota troops defeated the Dakota (who were not united in their decision to rebel) and hastily tried, convicted, and sentenced to death more than 300 Dakota men. Upon the intervention of Episcopal Bishop Henry B. Whipple, President Abraham Lincoln pardoned all but 38 of the men; the 38 were hanged at Mankato in the largest mass execution in U.S. history.

The military marched Dakota women, children, and old men some 150 miles to Fort Snelling, where they were contained over the winter of 1862–63 before banishment to reservations in South Dakota and Nebraska. A few Dakota people remained in the Twin Cities area, disguising their heritage.

Not until almost a century later did Dakota people return to their lands in and near the Longfellow neighborhood. In the meantime, poets and artists romanticized them in poems such as Longfellow's *Song of Hiawatha*, and officials named parks, roads, and schools Minnehaha and Hiawatha, only hinting at the past.

Minnehaha Avenue— The Road to Fort Snelling

The Indians established a trail from their villages at the confluence of the Mississippi and Minnesota Rivers to the Falls of St. Anthony along a slight ridge. The soldiers at Fort Snelling were the first new settlers to make regular use of that trail. In the early 1820s, the soldiers built a sawmill and a gristmill at St. Anthony Falls on the west side of the river, near today's downtown Minneapolis. Because the river nearby was too shallow and rocky for hauling goods by boat, the mills used that Indian trail, later called Old Territorial Trail, now Minnehaha Avenue. By the 1850s it was about 70 feet wide. Some of the earliest rail lines in Minnesota lay adjacent to this trail connecting Minneapolis and St. Paul to points south.

In 1875, much to the dismay of longtime residents, Minneapolis allowed the vacation of Old Territorial Road north of 28th Street so that the Chicago, St. Paul and Milwaukee Railroad could build its shops and roundhouse there. By 1930, the connection between Lake and 28th Streets ended with construction of the Minneapolis-Moline tractor factory. Not until redevelopment of rail yards in the early 1990s was the historic connection north of 28th Street reestablished.

What's in a Name?

Snelling

Fort Snelling and Snelling Avenue, which runs one block west of and parallel to Minnehaha Avenue, are the namesakes of Col. Josiah Snelling (1782–1828). Snelling served in the War of 1812, being promoted to the rank of colonel in 1820. His first assignment at that rank was to establish Fort St. Anthony at the juncture of the Mississippi and Minnesota Rivers. He oversaw the construction of the fort, completed in 1825; the army renamed it in his honor. Snelling and his wife, Abigail, had five children; she established a Sunday school for the fort's children. Colonel Snelling served as fort commander until his health started to decline in 1827. Forced to leave the fort, he moved to Washington, D.C., where he died in 1828.

◀ Josiah Snelling, c. 1820

White Settlement Begins

In the early 1850s, the land in what became Longfellow was still part of the Fort Snelling military reservation. The Traverse des Sioux Treaty of 1851 opened land to the west of the reservation to white settlement, increasing pressure to sell excess portions of the military acres. In anticipation, squatters descended on the military reservation, claiming nearly two-thirds of the land in the neighborhood by the end of 1852. By the end of 1853, nearly three-quarters of the land was spoken for.

◀ The old government flour mill and sawmill at the Falls of St. Anthony, 1857

Early Settlement

The U.S. War Department finally agreed to sell the land early in 1853. In July and August of that year the land that now is Longfellow was surveyed according to the township-and-range system used for most of the United States. The survey divided the land into standard units with descriptions of the land and vegetation to ready the land for sale. Meanwhile, those who had staked claims worried that a rush of claim jumpers would ruin their plans. So after much lobbying, Congress passed the Pre-emption Act, in March 1855, limiting the sale of the land to those who had claimed it earlier. The squatters had to supply statements from their neighbors detailing the date of the claim and any improvements. These affidavits, which enabled the claimants to buy the land without incident, provide invaluable information about the early settlement of the area.

1853 Government Land Survey map showing Longfellow east of 31st Avenue and south of Lake Street. At the bottom is Minnehaha Creek, then known as Brown's Creek. ▶

Township N.º 28 N, Range N.º 23 West.

- Large islands in the Mississippi, surveyed and sold just like other land
- Large marshy area "unfit for cultivation"
- Road to Fort Snelling (now Minnehaha Avenue)

Early Settlement Life

The early white settlers literally carved their homesteads out of the landscape: they had to be self-reliant. When the settlers came in 1852 to stake their claims, Minnesota was still a territory, the town of Minneapolis did not exist, and the settlement of St. Anthony boasted only a thousand hardy residents. Supplies from the outside world arrived in St. Paul by steamboat when the Mississippi wasn't frozen, so residents of the area raised or gathered as much of their food as they could. The only established road was that between Fort Snelling and the Falls of St. Anthony, and settlers with claims off the road had to make their way through tall prairie grass and scattered oak trees to reach their claims.

Hezekiah Atwood was one of the first settlers in what is now the Longfellow neighborhood. He staked his claim of 158 acres along the Mississippi River between today's 34th and 38th Streets and 42nd Avenue in March 1852. The potential for waterpower from the Mississippi River and Minnehaha Creek likely attracted this former machinist to that site. Atwood and his family lived in the area until 1856.

22 ■ The Neighborhood by the Falls

Below is an account of their time in the neighborhood that Atwood's daughter Jennie wrote more than 50 years after she lived there. The Wass girls she played with were Lizzie and Anness, featured later in this chapter.

> In the spring [of 1852] my father [Hezekiah] took up land and built a house down by the river not far from the Minnehaha Falls. He began to work on the Godfrey mill at Minnehaha. My mother [Abby Tuttle] was very timid. The sight of an Indian would nearly throw her into a fit. You can imagine that she was having fits most of the time, for they were always around. Timber wolves, too, were always skulking around and following the men, but I never knew them to hurt anyone. Father said it used to make even him nervous to have them keep so near him. They would be right close up to him, as close as a dog would be. He always took a lively gait and kept it all the time.
>
> One night father was a little late and mother had seen more terrifying things than usual during the day, so she was just about ready to fly. She always hated whip-poor-wills for she said they were such lonesome-feeling things. This night she stood peering out, listening intently. Then she, who tried so hard to be brave, broke into wild lamentations, saying she knew the wolves or Indians had killed father, and she would never see him again. My grandmother [Mary Tuttle] tried to calm her, but she would not be comforted until father came, then he had a great time getting her settled down. She said the whip-poor-wills seemed to say as she looked out in the blackness of the night, "Oh, he's killed—Oh, he's killed."
>
> What these timid town-bred women, used to all the comforts of civilization, suffered as pioneers, can never be fully understood. After that, whenever father was late, little as I was, and I was only four, I knew what mother was going through and would always sit close to her and pat her.
>
> Our home only had a shake roof, and during a rain it leaked in showers. My little sister [Emma] was born just at this time during an awful storm. We thought it would kill mother, but it did not seem to hurt her.
>
> The Indians used to come and demand meat. All we had was bacon. We gave them all we had, but when they ate it all up they demanded more. We were much frightened, but they did not hurt us. Father used to tap the maple trees, but we could not get any sap, for the Indians drank it all. That winter we lived a week on nothing but potatoes.
>
> Our nearest neighbor was Mrs. Wass. She had two little girls about our ages. They had come from Ohio. We used to love to go there to play and often did so. Once when I was four, her little girls had green and white gingham dresses. I thought them the prettiest

◀ Dakota men posing before Minnehaha Falls, 1857

things I had ever seen and probably they were, for we had little. When mother undressed me that night, two little green and white scraps of cloth fell out of the front of my little low-necked dress. Mother asked at once if Mrs. Wass gave them to me, and I had to answer, "No."

"Then," she said, "in the morning you will have to take them back and tell Mrs. Wass you took them."

I just hated to and cried and cried. In the morning, the first thing, she took me by the hand and led me to the edge of their plowed field and made me go on alone. When I got there, Mrs. Wass came out to meet me.

I said, "I've come to bring these."

She took me up in her arms and said, "You dear child, you are welcome to them."

But my mother would not let me have them. I never took anything again.

We had a Newfoundland dog by the name of Sancho, a most affectionate, faithful beast. A neighbor who had a lonely cabin borrowed him to stay with his wife while he was away. Someone shot him for a black bear. No person was ever lamented more.

Early Settlers

More than half of the original 20 settlers in the Longfellow neighborhood were from New England states, notably Maine. This was the case in the 1850s for Minnesota Territory as a whole. These New Englanders brought a distinct culture, working quickly to establish institutions and elements of civilization such as colleges and churches. They were naturally attracted to the waterpower of the Falls of St. Anthony, as waterpower was used extensively in New England.

Many of the original settlers in the neighborhood were farmers claiming land with intent to farm it, but many others quickly sold their land to speculators or held onto it for speculative purposes without living on it. Most of the speculative land, along the river, was less suitable for farming but attractive for its potential waterpower. And if navigation could be extended above St. Paul, the area would become prime real estate for boat landings and perhaps a new city. Most of the farmers stayed in the neighborhood well into the 1860s, but most of the speculators left due to bank foreclosures after the Panic of 1857.

Farmer Henry Keith and speculator Dorwin Moulton are representative of the early neighborhood settlers.

Henry Clay Keith

Henry Clay Keith (1823–1888) is typical of the New England farmers who staked their claims to establish farms in the neighborhood. Keith moved from Vermont to Minnesota Territory with his wife, Ruth, and young son, Albert, in the fall of 1853. In early 1855 he rushed to stake a claim along the Mississippi River in what is now the Seward and Longfellow neighborhoods. His claim was just south of the one his older brother, Asa, had staked in July 1854.

Henry Keith rushed to make his claim in the dead of winter, as the government was to sell the land including both brothers' claims later that year. In the space of two days in February 1855 he hastily constructed a rough, 12-foot-by-14-foot, two-room lean-to with a shed roof and two windows. There, near the bank of the Mississippi across from Meeker Island, he immediately moved with his pregnant wife and four-year-old son. The Keiths brought only meager furnishings—a wood stove, a bed, and a few tables.

Henry Clay Keith, c. 1885 ▶

That spring, Henry Keith broke one acre of the land to begin farming the homestead. In September 1855 a daughter, Mary, was born. Another son, John, was born in 1858, and about that time the family relocated to a new, larger house about half-a-mile away. Henry was an early trustee of the Free Will Baptist Church and lived close to an early church pastor, Rev. Charles G. Ames.

By 1860 Henry Keith had a relatively prosperous farm. Much of his claim, in Longfellow extending from 31st to 38th Avenues between 26th and 28th Streets, was oak savanna, which discouraged row crops but favored grazing and animal husbandry. In 1860 Keith had four milk cows, from which he produced a sizable amount of butter and cheese, and 14 pigs. The row crops he grew seem to have been for family subsistence and feed. Keith did not serve in the Civil War but did assist with the transport of goods to Fort Ripley and to the settlers in southern Minnesota caught in the Dakota War of 1862.

As the children came of school age, the family decided to move into town. In 1867 Keith sold his land, sawed the family home into three pieces, and moved it across the prairie to First Avenue North near Washington Avenue, in back of the Free Will Baptist Church (now the warehouse district of Minneapolis). After the move, he worked as a carpenter and operated a boardinghouse, despite his poor health. At the end of his life, Henry Keith lived with his daughter, Mary, and son-in law, Eufanant Merrill, a wealthy lawyer. Henry died in 1888, Ruth ten years later. Both are buried in Lakewood Cemetery.

Dorwin Moulton

Unlike Henry Keith, Dorwin E. Moulton (1822–1892) was a speculator and businessman who made his claim based on its proximity to the Mississippi. Moulton came to St. Anthony in 1851 from the lead-mining regions of southern Wisconsin and quickly became a leading St. Anthony businessman. Upon his arrival, he purchased the St. James Hotel in St. Anthony, and a few years later he was among the investors who built the first Hennepin Avenue Bridge across the Mississippi. One of the first people to claim land in the neighborhood, he staked 124 acres along the river, from Lake Street to 26th Street, in June 1852. By the end of October 1852, he had built a relatively substantial, two-story, wood-frame house. Although not in its original location, one section of the current home at 2832 Dorman is almost certainly the two-story home Moulton built in 1852, making it the oldest house in the neighborhood.

◀ Dorwin Moulton, c. 1880

During most of the early to mid-1850s, Moulton continued as a merchant residing in St. Anthony, hiring someone to live on his claim and keep it secure from jumpers. Moulton appears to have been the most active in the organizing and promoting of Falls City. After Falls City was laid out in 1857, he moved to the new town with his wife, Pamelia (Gardner), and daughter, Bell. He also set up a transfer company with Henry Keith to receive and forward goods by steamboat to the new port of Falls City. His time there was short. After the Panic of 1857 he moved back to St. Anthony, and in 1862 he left Minnesota altogether for Belvidere, Illinois, his wife's hometown. He worked there as a grocer until his death in 1892.

Falls City

Advertisement in the *Minnesota Republican*, August 13, 1857. Moulton and Keith were open for business in Falls City barely two weeks after the platting of the town. ▶

Plat map of Falls City, July 31, 1857 ▼

In 1850s territorial Minnesota, steamboats could easily reach St. Paul but not much farther upstream. Minneapolis and St. Anthony businessmen and boosters were eager to extend navigation as close to Minneapolis as possible. The Falls of St. Anthony prevented boats from docking near Minneapolis or St. Anthony, and the river was rough to a point just below Meeker Island (around the area in which the Short Line Bridge at 27th Street is today).

In early 1857, a group of 26 prominent men of trade and commerce, led by Bradley B. Meeker, incorporated the Mississippi River Improvement and Manufacturing Company. The company was to establish a system of locks and dams in the two-mile stretch of the river from the falls to where Lake Street is now. That would make it more navigable and break St. Paul's monopoly on steamboat traffic.

In this area the town of Falls City was laid out in the summer of 1857. Following the Mississippi from present-day Lake Street north almost to 24th Street and west to 38th Avenue along Lake Street and proceeding northwest in a zigzag to 33rd Avenue, it was to be a new port on the river. The town had more than 600 lots and easily could have accommodated several thousand people. The name Falls City probably comes from the steamship of the same name, commissioned in 1855 to run in the shallow river north of St. Paul. Of the five men laying out the new city, Dorwin Moulton and Henry Keith owned the most land platted for the town. Two weeks after making it official on July 31, 1857, Moulton and Keith began advertising themselves as shipping agents out of Falls City. At the height of its population in the summer of 1857, probably only two families—Keith and Moulton, totaling eight people—lived in Falls City.

All the grand schemes abruptly came to an end with the Panic of 1857. Reaching its height in mid-October 1857, the panic was one of the most severe economic crises in U.S. history. The subsequent economic depression lasted nearly two years and the national economy did not fully recover before the start of the Civil War in 1861. Any dreams of Falls City becoming a metropolis and a port on the Mississippi were dashed. Only a few lots had sold, and there was no hope for more. Moulton sold his Falls City land at the peak of the panic to banker Dorlon B. Dorman and retreated to St. Anthony. Dorman vacated his portion of Falls City in 1863, declaring that the plat of lots was "useless for the purposes for which they are laid out." Keith vacated his portion in 1866, moved into town, and a year later sold out. Today the only evidence of the paper metropolis is the layout of a few blocks in the Seward neighborhood.

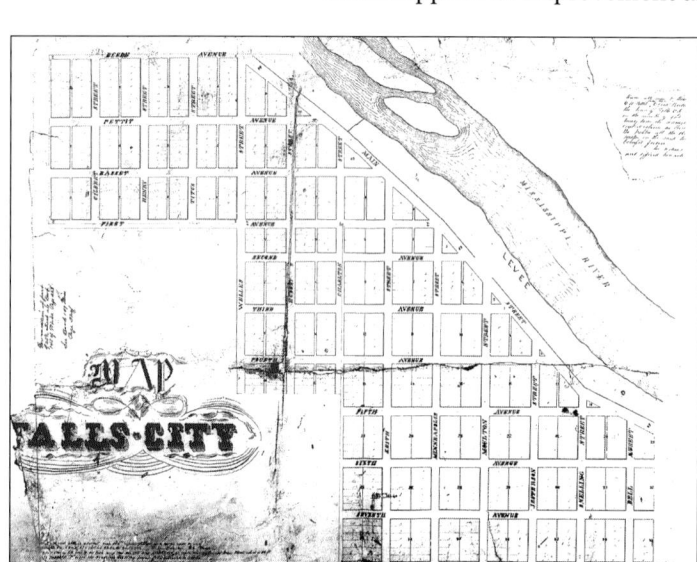

What's in a Name?

Dorman

Dorman Avenue, which runs north of Lake Street and one block west of and parallel to West River Parkway, is the namesake of the Dorman family, namely banker Dorlon B. Dorman (1825–1863). The avenue runs through the Falls City land that Dorwin Moulton sold to Dorlon Dorman in 1857. Dorman died in 1863 from the effects of an 1859 hunting accident on his property. None of his family ever lived on his land. His wife, Anna, and two children, Dorance and Mary (later Greer), divided the land into lots in 1885. Dorman's Addition goes from Lake to 26th Streets, 38th Avenue to the Mississippi River.

The Wass Sisters, Physicians

Nearly a century ago, when women comprised a tiny fraction of all physicians, the amazing Wass sisters, Anness and Lizzie, practiced medicine in Minneapolis. The Wass family, despite its humble beginning in the early days of the neighborhood, produced these extraordinary women who practiced much of their adult lives in Minneapolis and Los Angeles.

The sisters' parents, John and Eliza Wass, married in Indianapolis in early 1850. Anness was born there in December 1850. With the prospect of land opening for settlement in Minnesota Territory, the Wass family made the long steamboat journey on the Ohio and Mississippi Rivers as far as was possible to St. Anthony in 1851. The Wass family stayed in St. Anthony about a year; then in October 1852 John Wass made a claim on 156 acres bordered by what are now Lake and 34th Streets, 38th Avenue and the Mississippi.

John Wass quickly built a 12-foot-by-14-foot log cabin on the property; a few years later he added a more substantial, 12-foot-by-16-foot, wood-frame house. These houses were the equivalent of only two bedrooms in a 1920s Longfellow bungalow. The Wasses carved their homestead out of the scattered oaks and prairie just south today's Lake Street and a few blocks west of the Mississippi. Daughter Lizzie was born on their homestead in August 1854. The nearest neighbors were about half-a-mile away, but wild animals (even wolves) still roamed the area, and the Wasses likely interacted with Dakota people passing through the area. John Wass in 1860 tended his 27-acre farm, raising enough crops and livestock to support his family.

If Lizzie and Anness went to school, they had a long walk to Minneapolis, to St. Anthony, or to the school on Minnehaha Avenue near today's 46th Street. Anness and Lizzie were the only children of John and Eliza, and the family stayed together through many moves. The Wasses

◀ D. B. Dorman issued this paper currency in St. Anthony, September 30, 1862. At the beginning of the Civil War, coins and bills of small denomination were scarce. To make up for the shortage, bankers like Dorman issued their own currency.

◀ Anness and Lizzie Wass, 1882 class photos, Women's Medical College of Chicago

Early Settlement ■ 27

lived on their homestead until the late 1860s, when they moved to Napa County in northern California; there John took up farming again. They lived about ten years in northern California before heading back to the Midwest.

> **In the first group of physicians to be licensed by the state in 1883, they were two of only seven licensed women physicians, with several hundred male colleagues.**

The next stop was Chicago, where Lizzie and Anness enrolled in the Women's Medical College of Chicago in 1878. At the time, women could receive training in only a few women-only medical colleges, and this one was the closest to Minnesota. Medical school requirements were much less stringent then, and the sisters had to attend classes in Chicago for just one year. In 1879 the family returned to Minneapolis, where the sisters continued their training as interns with Hannibal H. Kimball, a prominent physician. The internships lasted three years, and Anness and Lizzie graduated in 1882.

The Wass sisters immediately started practicing medicine in Minneapolis and became involved in the Minnesota State Medical Society. In the first group of physicians to be licensed by the state in 1883, they were two of only seven licensed women physicians, with several hundred male colleagues.

Anness Wass had a general medicine and pediatrics practice while Lizzie specialized in nervous diseases and obstetrics. Lizzie is reported to have "studied and done original work in medical electricity." Unlike many of their male colleagues, the sisters never kept an office outside their home. The family moved often, living no closer to the original Wass homestead than in two houses in Seward, near 26th Avenue and 24th Street. Nevertheless, the Wasses left their mark on the neighborhood in the Wass Addition, divided into lots by the sisters in 1887 on the old homestead near the Mississippi at Lake Street.

In 1901, the family again packed up and moved to California, this time to Los Angeles. John and Eliza were by then in their early seventies, and both died a few years later. Lizzie and Anness continued to practice medicine together from the same house. Anness died at age 66 in 1917; Lizzie practiced medicine until 1919, when she retired for reasons of health. At age 83 she died in poverty at a Los Angeles nursing home in 1937.

The Wass sisters overcame strong social norms to forge long careers of medical practice. Only in the past 25 years have women become physicians in large number. Anness and Lizzie blazed the trail a hundred years before them.

3/Longfellow in 1900

Longfellow in 1900

Longfellow at the turn of the 20th century felt much more like country than city. It had few of the urban amenities enjoyed today. Streets acquired curbs and sidewalks when there were "enough" houses on a block but waited for paving until decades later. Only a few blocks had city-provided water and sewer service.

Overleaf—
Minneapolis Steel and Machinery, Minnehaha Avenue and 29th Street, c. 1910

E. F. Griswold Pickling Company ad, 1898 ▶

Longfellow in 1900 was still on the edge of the city—it had much more farmland than development. The neighborhood contributed only about 1,800 people to the total Minneapolis population of 202,718. Most of the neighborhood housing construction, generally north of Lake Street and west of 34th Avenue, dated to the 1880s and early 1890s. Lake Street east to the Mississippi was a muddy mess much of the time, and only after the streetcar went all the way to the river in 1906 did that part of the neighborhood see appreciable development.

A good portion of Longfellow had been laid out in lots, but only a small number were developed before the Panic of 1893. The panic called housing construction to an abrupt halt, and the ensuing economic depression lasted through the 1890s. What industry there was in the area was abandoned or scaled back by the late 1890s.

But things would soon rebound. The extension of the electric streetcar along Minnehaha Avenue to Minnehaha Park in 1890 connected the area with the rest of the city and made development possible after things started picking up in about 1905. The routing of the streetcar through the 27th and Lake intersection and the early commercial development in that area led to its status as "downtown" Longfellow by the 1920s. While a good portion of the neighborhood was still agrarian, the stage was set for the development of a vibrant neighborhood with a full complement of industrial and commercial enterprise.

E. F. GRISWOLD, Manager.
E. F. GRISWOLD PICKLING CO.,
FACTORY: Minnehaha Avenue and Lake Street.
Pickles, Vinegar, Mustard, Sauer Kraut, Etc.
OUR SPECIALTY—Griswold's Horse Radish.

The E. F. Griswold Pickling Company is an excellent example of a business in transition from agrarian edge to industrial part of the city. Edward F. Griswold had a short-lived condiment-making business near Lake Street and Minnehaha Avenue about 1900. His "factory" was in a two-story house, where he also lived with his wife, Anna, and two sons. He probably grew his own produce for the pickling company, as the 1900 census shows him renting a farm. In the 1880s and 1890s he was a gardener living just outside the neighborhood.

The Neighborhood by the Falls

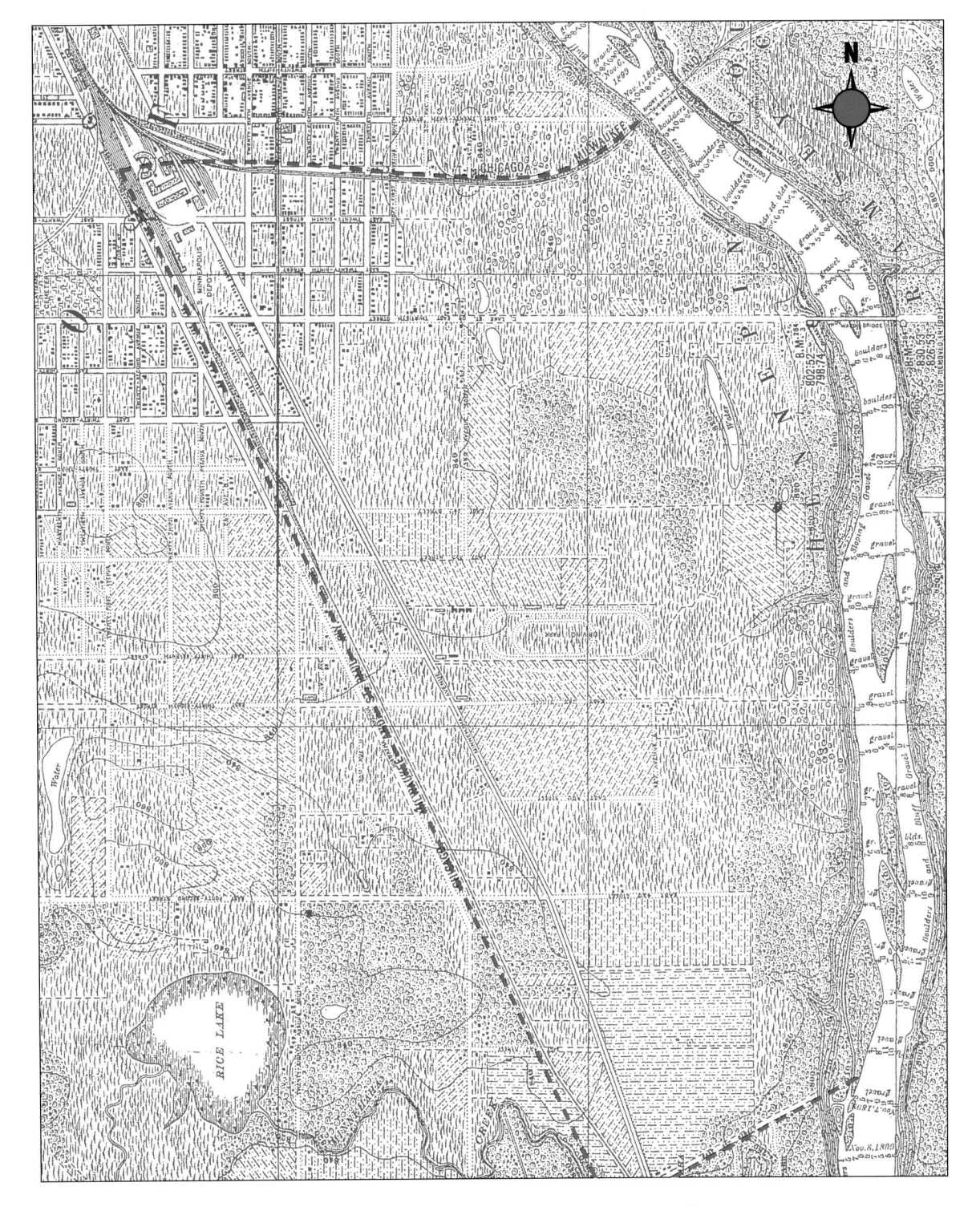

◀ Longfellow as it appeared in 1899 (outline) with the few established streets and houses concentrated north of Lake Street in the northwest portion of the neighborhood. The hatching patterns indicate land covers, such as fields or forest, unidentifiable without the lost map key.

Longfellow in 1900 ■ 31

Looking northwest from the top of the old Longfellow School, c. 1910. Note the muddy, rutted roads and overgrown landscape. E. F. Griswold had his pickling business at 2942 Minnehaha Avenue (the house at lower left). The first Longfellow Park is at upper right, just beyond the white house.

Residential Life in 1900

Longfellow at the turn of the 20th century felt much more like country than city. It had few of the urban amenities enjoyed today. Streets acquired curbs and sidewalks when there were "enough" houses on a block but waited for paving until decades later. Only a few blocks had city-provided water and sewer service. Most people had to provide their own with an outhouse out back and a well, likely shared with a neighbor. The streetcar running on 27th Avenue and then on Minnehaha ran on electricity, but residences didn't have that luxury. Some businesses had phones, but the simple homes in the neighborhood didn't have those, either. Those who could afford it and had the space to house them got around by horse and buggy. But most people took the streetcar or just walked.

These conditions weren't too different from those in other parts of the city, but fortunately for the folks in Longfellow, they had less chance of contracting diseases like cholera from unsanitary conditions. The houses in Longfellow were relatively far apart and the population was small enough that these diseases couldn't take hold.

32 ■ The Neighborhood by the Falls

The site at 2800 28th Avenue is a good example of the buildings and businesses developed during the booming 1880s and early 1890s. Grocer Orlando N. Gardner built the two-story portion in 1884 and the two additions later. He operated and lived above a grocery store there from 1884 to 1895, and in the early years of the 1890s he had a feed store as well. The Panic of 1893 put an end to it; he lost the building and store to foreclosure in 1895 and moved from the neighborhood.

Libby Family

One established household in 1900 was that of the Libby family, living near 31st Street and Minnehaha Avenue from the time of early white settlement well into the 20th century.

Maine native Allen Libby (1833–1911) was one of the earliest in the 27th and Lake area, settling along Minnehaha Avenue about a block south of Lake in 1860. That year he had a modest farm, growing grains such as wheat and other crops to feed his family. His obituary notes that he built his first house on the land, a "claim shanty," in 1864. In 1866 he married Hannah Garvey (1844–1902), also from Maine, and they had six children—sons Byron and Lewis and daughters Myrtle, Mabel, Viola, and Gertrude.

Allen Libby trained as a schoolteacher, and during most of the 1860s he taught in Hennepin County as well as farmed his land. He was involved in the community, serving on the school board of District 108, which built the predecessor of Longfellow School at Lake and Minnehaha in the mid-1870s. Libby was elected clerk of Minneapolis Township around 1880 and was the census taker for a portion of the township in 1880. He built a store on the southeast corner of Lake and Minnehaha in 1884, and he or his sons, Lewis and Byron, operated the store until about 1900.

In 1900 at the age of 66, Allen Libby had returned to his agrarian roots, as he appeared in that year's census as "gardener/farmer"; apparently, he grew vegetables and other crops for market. His oldest son, Byron (1867–1920), was confined to a wheelchair after having contracted spinal meningitis at age 16. Despite his disability, he started his own wood-and-coal fuel business in about 1900 and ran it until his death in 1920. Byron was also a neighborhood census taker in 1900—long before handicapped accessibility was remotely considered! In the early years of the 20th century, all six of the Libby children lived within one block of the old family homestead.

◀ 2841 29th Avenue, 2007. Built in 1884, this home is representative of simple folk-style houses built in Longfellow in the 1880s and common in the neighborhood in 1900.

◀ 2800 28th Avenue, 2007

◀ Libby House, 3107 28th Avenue, 2005

Hannah Libby died in 1902 and was buried at Oak Hill Cemetery in Minneapolis. Allen Libby retired in 1906, and in 1909 his house was moved from its original location at the northeast corner of 31st Street and Minnehaha Avenue to its present site at 3107 28th Avenue. He died in 1911 and was buried at Oak Hill Cemetery in Minneapolis.

Longfellow School

In 1900, there was only one school in the neighborhood—Longfellow, on the northeast corner of Lake Street and Minnehaha Avenue, between Minnehaha and 27th Avenues. Three buildings built or moved to the site comprised the original Longfellow School. The first, built about 1876, was known for a time as Centennial School, apparently for the American Centennial, 1776–1876. At the time of its first incarnation, the school was outside city limits, under the jurisdiction of School District 108.

The first building was a two-story structure, about the size of a large house, of the Second Empire style common in the 1870s. Bigger than the one-room schoolhouses common in the township previously, it was not so large as those built in established parts of the city. In 1883, the area including the school became part of the city, and the school came under the jurisdiction of Minneapolis Public Schools. In that year the small school building reportedly held 191 students.

Longfellow School, c. 1910 (l to r): 1908 addition, 1887 building, original 1870s Centennial School ▶

Longfellow Field, 26th Avenue and 29th Street, 1912

Bessie Robinson, director of the Longfellow School kindergarten, 1899

With the school apparently needing more space, in 1885 the district moved a two-story brick building to the site, and the school took the name Longfellow. A population boom in the area during the mid-to-late 1880s led to the construction of a substantial three-story brick building in 1887. The new school was part of a building boom experienced by the Minneapolis Public Schools in the 1880s and early 1890s. As enrollment increased, a two-story addition, about half the size of the 1887 structure, further expanded the school in 1908.

About 1900 Longfellow School, under the leadership of teacher Bessie Robinson, was one of the first in the city to offer a kindergarten. It was also one of the first to organize a parent-teacher association.

The school's tiny playground was just south of Jake Martin's barn, and the story goes that whenever one of the kids' balls broke a window of the barn, the principal sent over a student to apologize and pay for a new window. Later, between 1911 and 1917, students used the playground at the first Longfellow Park. Located at 29th Street and 26th Avenue, where Cub Foods is today, it was the first official park in the neighborhood. In 1918 both park and school relocated to a more residential area, the school to a new building at 31st Avenue and 31st Street, still in use today.

Longfellow's First Fire Station—No. 21

Longfellow's first fire station arose at 3010 Minnehaha Avenue in 1894. Until 1901 the station had only a "chemical engine" company—nothing more than a big soda-acid fire extinguisher, the type used in outlying areas to hold a fire until steamers and hose wagons arrived from other stations. In the late 1890s, the vast majority of houses and stores in the neighborhood were within a few blocks of the station, and few new houses and buildings were under construction. As the neighborhood developed, a hose engine made its debut in 1901, followed by the ladder unit making it a full-scale fire station. In 1912, the station had 13 firefighters, seven horses, and a combined chemical and hose wagon.

During most of the fire station's existence, before the telephone was in widespread use, residents reported fires through alarm boxes placed around the neighborhood. In 1900 there were only five of these in Longfellow, most of them close to industrial and commercial areas. Only one was in a residential area. Even if one found an alarm box nearby, he or she still had to find out who had the key for the alarm.

Message of a fire reached the central dispatch station via high-tech telegraph, likewise from there to the closest station to dispatch the fire engine. The keyholder sounding the alarm was to further direct firefighters arriving on the scene. If the keyholder could not be found, the firefighters looked for smoke, no small task at a time when even the smallest building had a chimney belching the gray stuff. The widespread use of the telephone after World War II meant the demise of the alarm boxes in the early 1960s.

Fire Station No. 21, 3010 Minnehaha, 1936

The fire station remained at 3010 Minnehaha Avenue until 1961, when a new station opened at 38th Street and Snelling Avenue. A group called the "Firehouse Theater" used the old building for several years after the fire station closed. Minnehaha Furniture bought and used the building until 1999, when current owner Patrick Scully moved Patrick's Cabaret to the site.

Lauritzen Wagon and Blacksmith Shop

Martinus Nelson built a blacksmith shop at 3012 Minnehaha in 1888, a few years before the appearance of the fire station. At that time, the vast majority of the neighborhood was open farmland, and dairy cows dotted the landscape. The smithy serviced the local horses and wagons that kept the dairy farms running. Nelson lived in the rear of his shop with his family. In about 1893 he went into business with Charles Jeppeson, who moved in next door.

By far the longest owner of the business was Christian Lauritzen, who took over about 1898. Lauritzen emigrated from Denmark to the United States in 1893, and by the time he moved with his wife, Hilleborg, into the back of the blacksmith shop, they had two young children. He built a more substantial shop with a brick facade in 1904, and five years later he moved his home from the back of the shop to 3136 Minnehaha, where he lived the rest of his life. Lauritzen's modest brick home is standing today. Despite the rise of the automobile and resulting paucity of horses in the area, he continued to operate a blacksmith shop at 3012 Minnehaha until his death in 1942.

Lauritzen witnessed huge changes during his time there, watching the area go from a small outpost on the edge of Minneapolis to a totally developed neighborhood with nary a horse. The building continued to house a blacksmith shop or ironworks after World War II, but by the mid-1950s it had become a storage area for Minnehaha Furniture and Carpet Company, its store at the southwest corner of Minnehaha Avenue and Lake Street.

◀ Lauritzen Wagon and Blacksmith Shop, 3012 Minnehaha Avenue, c. 1900

The simple brick building survived almost a hundred years until the mid-1980s, when it gave way to a parking lot for a new tenant in the upstairs of the old fire station, Airport Taxi.

Two dairyman's houses still standing in Longfellow—

2801 31st Avenue, Seierson house, 2008. Built in 1885, this was the home of Danish immigrant Mads Seierson, who probably had the last working dairy farm of the neighborhood, between 31st and 36th Avenues, 28th Street and the railroad tracks, from 1893 until his death in 1939. ▶

3320 31st Street, 2008, built c. 1885. Danish immigrant Andrew Larsen lived here in 1900; he had been in the area since about 1887. ▶

Dairyland

As early as 1880, Danish immigrant Hans Johanson operated a dairy farm near the Mississippi River south of Lake Street; the number of area dairy farms increased during the 1880s. The Panic of 1893 brought home construction to a halt, rendering the land more suitable for small-scale dairy farming. The available land and the ample supply of new Scandinavian immigrants set the stage for a boom in dairying in the 1890s.

The year 1900 saw about 15 dairy farmers and their families scattered across the neighborhood from 28th Street and 31st Avenue to 46th Street and 46th Avenue. Dairy farms ranged in size from 5 to 50 cows with the average about 25. In 1903, the total size of the Longfellow dairy "herd" was about 500 head. In comparison, in 2007, nearly half of Minnesota's dairy farms had 50 to 99 head. Today, 40 percent of Minnesota's dairy farms are about the size of Longfellow's at the turn of the 20th century.

... a dairy farmer could buy a standard city lot, build his house and barn, blaze a trail to the house, and graze his cows on the surrounding undisturbed land.

Though real estate development in Longfellow came to a halt by 1900, large tracts of vacant land remained. Recent immigrants, mostly from the Scandinavian countries of Sweden, Denmark, and Norway, saw the open expanses as opportunities for small-scale dairy farming. Some had dairying experience in their home countries, and the real estate speculators holding most of the vacant land were more than eager to rent the acres while they waited for another building boom.

A good portion of the neighborhood, especially land east of 34th Avenue, retained its pre-settlement native landscape—scattered oak trees on prairie with scattered wetlands. In the early days of settlement, this landscape had discouraged the breaking of the prairie and large-scale row-crop farming as settlers would have had to clear stumps and fill swamps to get a good-sized farm. But the ample grass, trees for shade, water, and open areas for growing fodder made the land ideal for raising and keeping dairy cattle. The subsequent dairy farms owed their existence on the edge of the growing city to the particular process of development there.

Land development in the 19th century was far from what it is today. The modern developer clears land for division into lots, putting in streets and utilities well before house construction begins. In the 19th century, it was just the opposite. Land remained untouched until lots were sold and houses built. Grading, but not paving, and sidewalks were next. In the neighborhood closest to the river such as Dorman's Addition (38th Avenue to the River, Lake to

26th Streets), large areas could be laid out in lots, but since few homes were built, no streets were put in; neither did clearing of the land occur.

Paradoxically, a dairy farmer could buy a standard city lot, build his house and barn, blaze a trail to the house, and graze his cows on the surrounding undisturbed land. There was no expectation of modern utilities (water, sewer, electricity), so it was easy to set up a small farmstead in the middle of the scattered oak trees and prairie.

Most dairy farms located on the edge of more developed areas or near the Mississippi River, in small clusters with barns and, presumably, shared wells and farm equipment. In the northwest part of the neighborhood around 28th Street and 31st and 32nd Avenues was a cluster of several houses in which dairy farmers (among people with other occupations) lived. Just south of Lake at 31st Street along 34th Avenue were several dairyman houses. Large barns lined the east side of 34th Avenue.

Near the northeast corner of the neighborhood, a good number of dairymen's residences appeared along 41st and 42nd Avenues near 28th Street, not far from the Mississippi. South of there, along the river, dairies scattered to 46th Street. The last cluster, at the present intersection of 42nd Avenue and 38th Streets, was the origin of the small commercial district found in that area today.

Farmers fed their cows everything from grains such as millet and corn, to brewery waste such as mash, to weeds such as cockle. Some of the bigger operations with more land probably grew some of their feed, but none had enough land to grow all its feed and hay. A few of the smallest operations in the more settled parts of the neighborhood fed their cows exclusively on distillery waste such as mash and malt. Nearly all of Longfellow's dairy farmers were retail operators, meaning that they delivered fresh milk every day directly to residential customers. In the days before widespread refrigeration, this was the only way

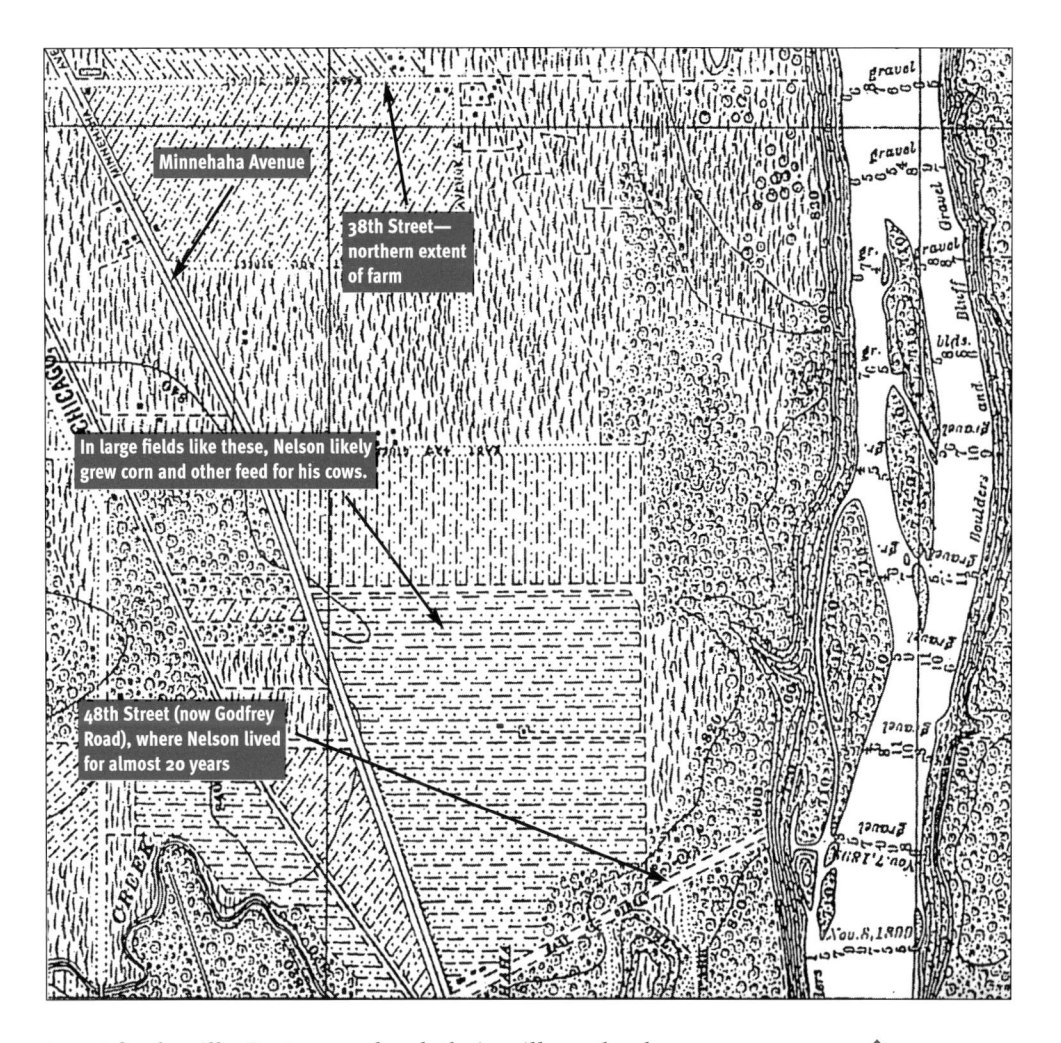

to get fresh milk. Customers drank their milk on the day of delivery and made leftovers into products such as fresh cheese.

Danish dairyman Martin Nelson had a farm at the southern end of the neighborhood near the intersection of 46th Avenue and 46th Street from 1894 to 1913. Under the name Minnehaha Dairy, he ran a wholesale operation, producing milk for local institutions such as the Minnesota Veterans Home (just south of Minnehaha

Extent of Nelson Dairy Farm, 1899

Rasmus Rasmussen, dairy farmer, delivering milk and cream, 1907. Rasmussen kept 20 dairy cows near 46th Street and Hiawatha Avenue. This photo illustrates how city and farm intermingled in the first years of the 20th century. ▶

Park) and Sheltering Arms, an orphanage at 44th and West River Parkway. His son Victor recalls that when his father first moved his herd to this part of the neighborhood, nobody knew who owned the land. So he just started grazing his cows and growing crops such as corn and potatoes.

Later the out-of-town owners agreed to lease their land to Nelson. His farm consisted of 40 cows and 90 acres from 38th to 48th Streets (now Godfrey Road) and Hiawatha Avenue to the the Mississippi River. Martin Nelson's dairy prospered for an unusually long time due to its location far from development.

Martin Nelson's dairy likely was the last of the larger-scale dairies in Longfellow. Between 1900 and 1910 Minneapolis's population increased by 50 percent, driven by a large influx of immigrants during which development in Longfellow took off. Home construction filled previously empty subdivisions, and land speculators subdivided even more land for homes. As large tracts of vacant land disappeared, development pushed the dairy farms pushed farther to the south until they were out of the city completely. Today the only reminders of Longfellow's dairyland are the homes of the farmers blending into the urban landscape.

The Slumlord of 27½ Street

Longfellow, a neighborhood of small, single-family houses, had few of the dense and poverty-ridden tenements common in Chicago and other eastern cities in the early 1900s. An exception was the small group of row houses at the northwestern corner of the neighborhood developed by the unlikely slumlord Gen. Eli L. Huggins.

Eli Huggins's father, Rev. Alexander G. Huggins, came to Minnesota in 1835 as an Indian missionary, and he was the first white settler in Nicollet County, Minnesota (near Mankato). After briefly attending Hamline University in St. Paul, Eli volunteered for the Civil War, at age 18 part of the first group of Minnesota volunteers in 1861.

He fought in many battles and by 1866 earned the rank of first lieutenant.

Huggins spent the majority of his military career in "Indian Territory" and on various Indian campaigns. In 1894 he received the Congressional Medal of Honor for his efforts in a relatively minor battle against the Dakota in Montana in 1880. His father and two of his brothers in Nicollet County died in Minnesota's Dakota War of 1862, which probably influenced his decision to continue service. He never married and moved often, as is typical for a military man. General Huggins lived in Minnesota only briefly, from 1872 to 1875, when he fulfilled an assignment teaching military science at the University of Minnesota. Just before his retirement in 1903, he received the rank of "Brigadier General, 2nd US Calvary, Indian Wars."

During his time in Minnesota, Huggins purchased the lots where the 27½ Street tenements would be built. He purchased the lots in 1874 in the first subdivision in the neighborhood—South Minneapolis. In 1874 the neighborhood was almost exclusively farmland, with only a few houses and the newly built Minneapolis Harvester Works near Lake and Minnehaha.

Huggins built a group of nine attached tenement houses on just one lot near 27th Avenue in the early 1880s. This and another block of houses faced the interior of the lot rather than the street, as most houses did, so he had to find another of way of access to the units. He used two of his lots to create 27½ Street between 27th and 28th Avenues, just north of 28th Street. He neglected to make the street official, which would have meant spending money on sidewalks and curbs, so there was little more than a dirt path. Across the dirt path and towards 28th Avenue, Huggins developed another lot with five (barely) detached houses. In all, 27½ Street had 16 housing units on three lots, more than five times the density of the surrounding single-family houses.

The attached tenement houses near 27th Avenue were the size of a modest two-bedroom bungalow in the neighborhood but had many large families packed into the space. Because of the poverty of the tenants, many grown children commonly lived in the houses there, helping to support the family even after they had families of their own. While the number of people in each unit was not unusual, the number of units on each lot was. Some tenants were immigrants; many were born in the United States but had foreign-born parents. They held common working-class jobs of the time—as laborers, factory workers, painters, carpenters, and so forth.

Huggins retired to Oklahoma (former Indian Territory) in 1903 and sold the tenements to James Reid, a local real estate man, who apparently carried on the slumlord

◀ Eli L. Huggins, c. 1903

Huggins properties, 1892 (circled). Some maps showed Lots 9 and 16 as 27½ Street. Note the solid row of tenements on Lot 17. ▶

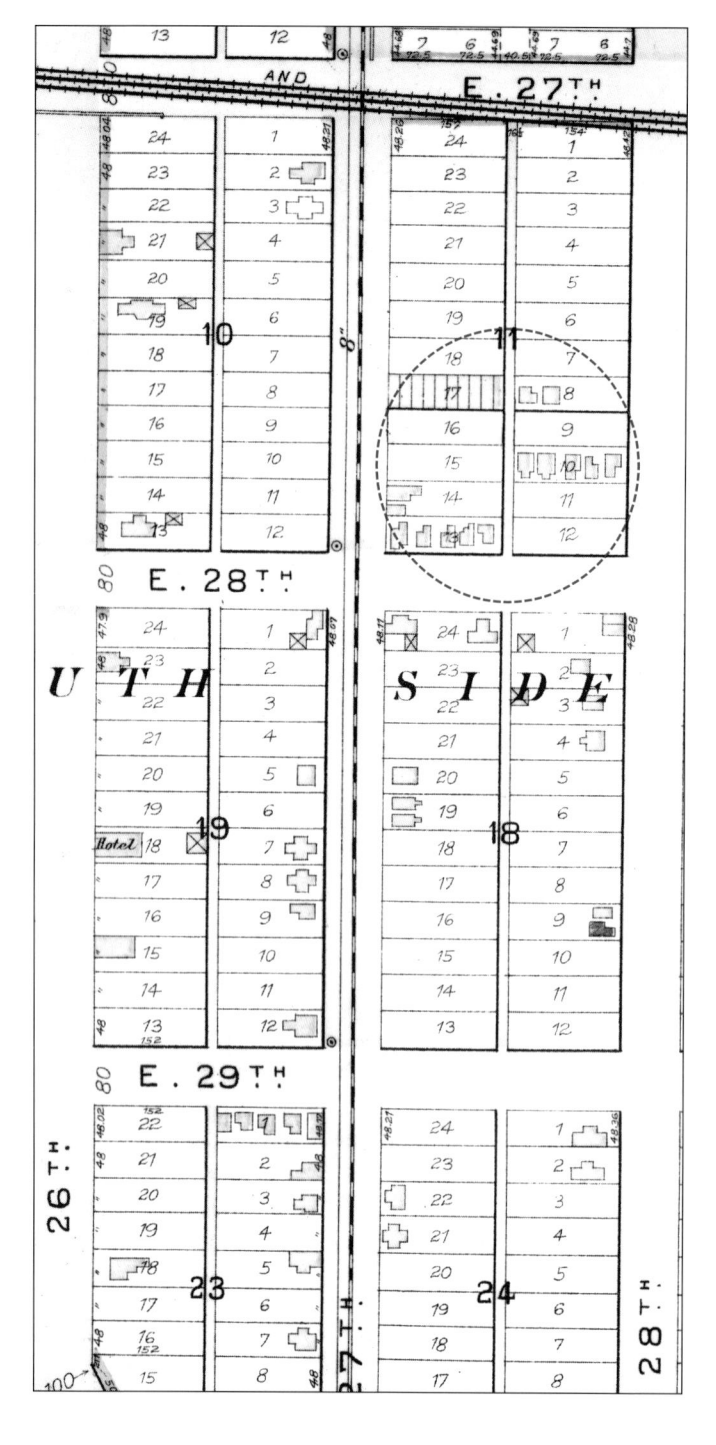

tradition. By the 1920s, the dilapidated tenements attracted the attention of social reformers. The Women's Co-Operative Alliance, a well-organized reform group, produced a report in 1926 on the social and housing conditions of south Minneapolis, singling out 27½ Street as a problem:

> Two blocks north of Lake Street is a narrow alley-like street, one block long, not indicated on city maps. The houses are wretched, old buildings, most of them built close to the sidewalk and housing several families. There are no yards. An alley runs back of the houses and is the only space between the rear doors and a high board fence. The street is uncurbed, unpaved, and dirty. At the east end of the block is a little more space but it is cluttered with unsightly sheds and salvage. Chickens and animals are kept close to the houses.

Worse yet, the caption under a small photo in the report read: "27½ Street Looking east from 27th Avenue. Dirty, cluttered, and unpaved. Houses wretched, close to street. Colored and white people." So much for racial integration.

The tenements gave way to expanding industry in the area shortly afterward. In about 1929, Northwestern Tile and Marble, which had a large plant just to the north of the site, bought the lots on either side of 27½ Street to expand its business, wiping out the tenements. The mid-1970s saw further redevelopment replacing the remaining single-family homes and old buildings with the industrial structures that stand today.

42 ■ The Neighborhood by the Falls

4 /Social Life

Social Life

The first white immigrants to settle in Longfellow were native-born New Englanders arriving in the 1850s to establish farmsteads. By 1900, nearly all of the new residents were immigrants from the Scandinavian countries of Sweden, Denmark, and Norway. These groups and other social service agencies established orphanages, nursing homes, and other institutions in the early 20th century.

Overleaf—
Danish Young People's Home soccer team, c. 1925

Round Table Club members playing with children at Sheltering Arms, just one of the many social service agencies in the neighborhood, 1926 ▶

The first white immigrants to settle in Longfellow were native-born New Englanders arriving in the 1850s to establish farmsteads. As the land was divided into lots in the 1870s, more people moved into the neighborhood. The newcomers were still mostly native-born, but they came from all points east as well as from midwestern states such as Ohio and Indiana.

The first waves of foreign-born residents showed up in the mid-1880s. By 1900, nearly all of the new residents were immigrants from the Scandinavian countries of Sweden, Denmark, and Norway.

These immigrants lived in the new houses (and a few tenements) popping up around 27th and Lake and on the dairy farms at the edges of the city.

By 1910, Swedes made up the single largest ethnic group in Minneapolis, dominating the south-side neighborhoods

44 ■ The Neighborhood by the Falls

Longfellow remained an overwhelmingly white neighborhood for much of the 20th century. The number of persons of color (mostly African Americans) by mid-century was considerably less than 1 percent of the total, and even by 1970 it was only 2 percent. One notable exception is the African-American community that developed early in the 20th century along Snelling Avenue. The number of persons of color living in the neighborhood rose dramatically between 1990 and 2000, from 9 percent to 20 percent as African immigrants and Hispanics moved into the western parts of the neighborhood, especially along Minnehaha Avenue. In 2000, the neighborhood was 80 percent Caucasian, 8 percent African American, 6 percent Hispanic, and 6 percent other.

◀ Auditorium, Minnehaha Academy, ca. 1925. Swedish immigrants who saw the need for a Christian high school for second-generation Swedes started Minnehaha Academy in 1912.

like Longfellow. The average Longfellow block included families with names such as Anderson and Peterson, of Swedish, Norwegian, or Danish descent. In the first few decades of the 20th century, half of all the residents had been born in one of these Scandinavian countries or had a parent or parents born there. The Swedes and Danes established institutions for their own in the neighborhood. The Swedes founded a Christian high school—Minnehaha Academy—and the Danes both a nursing home—Danebo—and the Danish Young People's Home.

The area along the Mississippi River, the last to be developed and the most available, became home to several orphanages and early social service agencies.

The population of the neighborhood peaked at about 28,000 in 1940, and it has declined since. In 2000 about 21,000 people lived there, a decrease of 25 percent, consistent with citywide trends and mostly due to a decrease in household size. As baby boomers moved on and families became smaller, the population naturally dropped, without loss of housing stock in the neighborhood.

The area along the Mississippi River, the last to be developed and the most available, became home to several orphanages and early social service agencies. As land along the river was the last to be divided into lots, large tracts of land remained available for institutions such as schools and orphanages even into the late 1920s and early 1930s. Two orphanages, a nursing home, a private high school, and an elementary school for "crippled" children were established close to the Mississippi before the land became more valuable for residential development.

Social Life ■ 45

Danish Young People's Home 1918–1966

In 1918, Martin Nelson, a leader in the south Minneapolis Danish community, saw the need for a home, club, or gathering place for young people who came to the Twin Cities. He raised enough money to buy the 1889 Moffett mansion and move it a few hundred feet down 42nd Street from Minnehaha, to 3620 East 42nd Street. There he established the Danish Young People's Home, providing room and board for about 20 young people as well as a gathering place for the local Danish community.

Housemaids came there for sing-alongs, parties, plays, and entertainment, and the tennis courts were popular. Many immigrants of the early 1920s met their future spouses at the home. Seventeen Danes, mostly men 25 to 35 years of age, lived at the Young People's home in 1920.

As time progressed, the need for this type of club for young Danes decreased. By the mid-1960s the home was little used and barely solvent. It closed in 1966, and within a few years the building was demolished. An apartment building constructed on the site still stands at 3620 East 42nd Street.

Danish Young People's Home soccer team, c. 1925

Martin Nelson, 1928 ▶

Danish Young People's Home (3620 East 42nd Street), drawing by Robert James Sorenson, 1968 ▶

46 ■ The Neighborhood by the Falls

Danebo Old People's Home, 3030–3034 West River Parkway, c. 1930

Danebo
1924–2005

Danebo, or "home of the Danes," was built in 1924 as a nursing home for elderly Danes on West River Parkway, just south of Lake Street. Established by a group of Twin Cities Danish organizations, it was nondenominational and open to Danish men and women from the Twin Cities regardless of income or assets. Martin Nelson, also instrumental in setting up the Danish Young People's Home, headed the effort to establish the home.

In its early days, the home set up "supporting circles," a volunteer and informal support network for its more needy residents. People donated vegetables to the home from their gardens during harvesting seasons and spent time at the home during the holidays with relatives or other Danes they knew there. Volunteers maintained the grounds and performed other services, keeping the home's costs low. Card games at private homes or at Danebo were popular fundraisers—players contributed a small amount to play, and all the money raised went to Danebo. Socializing and service came together to provide neighborhood Danes "a social life with a cause."

The founders of Danebo wanted their elderly fellow Danish immigrants to be as well cared for in America as was the case in Denmark. In a time before Social Security and other government programs for the elderly, Danebo offered a social support system and a nice place to stay regardless of ability to pay. Beyond its charitable events, the home raised money from a variety of sources (donations, county-aid checks, and so forth) to cover the expenses of those who could not afford to stay there.

Besides being a home for elderly Danes, Danebo served as social center of the Danish community, sponsoring events such as Sommerfest, which drew large crowds each year.

Residents of Danebo Old People's Home, c. 1950

In 1961, a major addition to the north end of the home nearly doubled its size. In the 1960s, the home opened its doors to other Scandinavians, and in the last years of its operation, Danebo had no Danish residents. A facility of fewer than 30 rooms, it could not compete with the larger and more modern nursing homes and services for seniors in the 21st century. The last resident moved out of Danebo on March 15, 2005; Danebo now serves as a Danish cultural center.

Snelling Avenue African-American Community

While the population of Longfellow has been overwhelmingly white for most of its history, a notable exception existed in a few blocks of Snelling Avenue, where an African-American and mixed-race community evolved during the first half of the 20th century.

The first resident of this area was John Monroe, a railroad cook who built his house at 3633 Snelling about 1905. The larger community, which developed only after the end of World War I in 1918, centered on the block where Monroe lived. The increase in Longfellow's black population coincided with the mass migration of blacks from the South to the nation's northern cities, driven by the demand for factory labor. Immigration from Europe had ceased with World War I, and northern factory owners recruited southern blacks to fill the positions that European immigrants had taken earlier.

One notable resident moving in around this time was Sylestus Phelps. Known for the "famous fried chicken" of her downtown Minneapolis café and her "Oh Boy Chicken Shack" at the Minnesota State Fair, Phelps lived at 3624 Snelling from 1917 to 1924. By the time of her death in 1944 Sylestus Phelps Williams reportedly was one of the wealthiest black women in the Twin Cities.

By 1920 about 15 black or mixed-race households occupied homes along Snelling Avenue within a few blocks of 36th Street. Members of this community worked in service occupations, such as railroad porter and chambermaid, typical for black and mixed-race people at the time. Most of them owned their modest homes, and many households included extended family members such as siblings or parents. By 1930, the number of African-American households had doubled to around 30, mostly in the 3500, 3600, and 3700 blocks of Snelling Avenue. These blocks along Snelling were one of the few truly integrated parts of the city, with some blocks almost evenly split with 40 percent black and 60 percent white residents.

The community endured after World War II, and the St. James African Methodist Episcopal (AME) Church built a new place of worship in the heart of the district at 3600 Snelling in 1959. Snelling Avenue between 34th and 39th Street continued as the only integrated section of the neighborhood until Hispanic and African immigrants started moving into the western part in the 1990s.

St. James AME Church, 3600 Snelling, 1975

◀ Children at Michael J. Dowling School for Crippled Children, c. 1925

Michael J. Dowling School for Crippled Children

During the 19th century and into the early decades of the 20th, physically challenged children in Minneapolis were educated at home, if at all. During the Progressive Era, around World War I, attitudes began to change and schools opened especially to educate these children.

In 1920, the Minneapolis Board of Education established a school for children with physical disabilities. The school, named after Michael J. Dowling (1866–1921), operated in a church building at 18th and Dupont Avenue North. Dowling was an educator and banker who overcame substantial disabilities to become a political leader in Minnesota after the turn of the 20th century. Caught as a boy of 14 in the blizzard of 1880, he endured the amputation of both legs just below the knee, of most of the fingers of his right hand, and of his left arm just below the elbow.

Social Life ■ 49

Soon after its establishment, Dowling School developed a broad base of community support for its educational mission. William Eustis, a former mayor of Minneapolis (1891–93), donated 21 acres on West River Parkway as well as the funding to build the school there. Like Dowling, Eustis had not been able to walk as a boy. A lawyer and real estate man, he quietly amassed a fortune, with the intention of giving it for the benefit of children with handicaps.

The new Michael J. Dowling School for Crippled Children opened at 3900 West River Parkway in 1924. Through the remaining 1920s and into the 1930s, the school expanded its programs and facilities.

A high point came on October 9, 1936, when President Franklin Roosevelt and his wife, Eleanor, came to the school to dedicate a new therapeutic swimming pool. A federal Works Progress Administration (WPA) grant funded the pool.

Roosevelt, crippled by polio in 1921, had a keen interest in aquatherapy as a treatment for his disease and other disabilities. In a brief speech to the crowd gathered on the school grounds, the president made an oblique reference to his own condition. Turning to the children, he said, "I hope all of you will be able to learn to swim in this fine pool. Swimming, as you know, is the only exercise I can take."

President and Eleanor Roosevelt visited Dowling School in 1936 to dedicate its new therapeutic pool. Minnesota's Gov. Hjalmar Petersen sat next to Eleanor Roosevelt. ▶

Over the succeeding decades, the school expanded, adding two new classroom wings, an auditorium, and a loading zone. At the school's 50th anniversary in 1974, Dowling was still identified as a "program for the physically handicapped." But that soon changed. As the mainstreaming movement gained momentum in the 1980s, many parents of disabled children began pressing to have their children educated in regular classrooms.

Dowling's history as a specialized school for physically challenged children ended in 1987 when the school reorganized to include children without physical disabilities. Taking advantage of its natural setting overlooking the Mississippi River gorge, Dowling is now an Urban Environmental Learning Center.

50 ■ The Neighborhood by the Falls

Lutheran Children's Friend Society

The Lutheran Children's Friend Society (LCFS), an early leader in the field of child welfare, operated an orphanage at 36th and Edmund Boulevard from 1924 until 1968. E. Buckley Glabe, its longtime superintendent, became a leader in the community as well.

The Lutheran Children's Friend Society, founded in Minnesota in 1901, was part of a larger regional organization including Lutheran Children's Friend Societies established in several midwestern states around that time. All were associated with the Lutheran Church-Missouri Synod. A child-welfare organization, the Minnesota society soon opened an orphanage at 2022 Marshall Avenue in St. Paul. In 1923 the society purchased three acres of land at 36th and Edmund, and by 1924 it had constructed its second such facility in the Twin Cities. An architect who had previously designed creameries drew plans for the two-story, Tudor-style building of brick and concrete. A matching home for the superintendent went up at the same time at 3624 Edmund Boulevard; it still stands today.

Rev. Edwin Buckley Glabe, called from a congregation in Sandstone, Minnesota, served as superintendent of the new orphanage. He spent much of his time on the road, visiting Lutheran congregations around the state to raise money and spread word of the society's work. He was superintendent (officially executive secretary) of LCFS for 40 years, retiring only after Lutheran Social Services took over the Lutheran Children's Friend Society in 1968, at which time the facility closed. Reverend Glabe died in 1969; hundreds attended the memorial service at Christ Church Lutheran for this much-loved man.

The LCFS orphanage, sometimes referred to as a "foundling" or "receiving" home, was primarily a place for the care of infants before adoption. Unmarried pregnant women could count on the society for support before their babies' births and for help in placing their children for adoption. The pastors of Lutheran churches outside the Twin Cities sometimes referred unwed pregnant women from their congregations to the home.

◄ Rev. E. Buckley Glabe, 1968

◄ Lutheran Children's Friend Society, 3606 West River Parkway, c. 1924. This side of the building faced Edmund Boulevard.

◄ This boy and girl eating at Lutheran Children's Friend Society, 1934, were some of the older orphans at the home.

Social Life

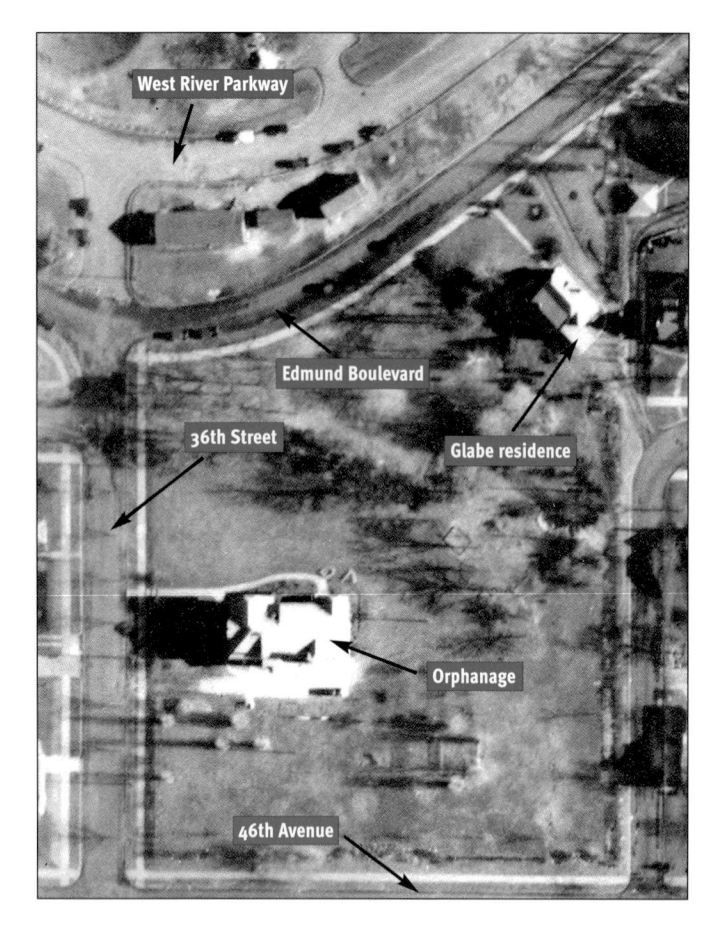

Lutheran Children's Friend Society site, 1938 ▶

In the early days of the orphanage, infants lived on the premises until suitable adoptive families could be found. LCFS took all the babies who came its way, including those considered hard to place. In 1930, the matron, three nursemaids, two social workers, a clinical worker, janitor, a cook, and a laundress (all living on site) were caring for 23 infants and toddlers at the orphanage.

At its 25th anniversary celebration in 1949, LCFS announced that the Minneapolis facility had provided shelter for more than 2,000 boys and girls. By the 1950s the home had become an adoption agency placing about 50 children each year; it no longer housed infants for any length of time. In the mid-1960s, the number of adopted infants topped 100 and was expected to rise dramatically with the increase in out-of-wedlock births in those days of "free love." Reverend Glabe ensured that the intense, personal, not-too bureaucratic adoption process culminated on a spiritual note by conducting a "placement service" for the families utilizing the agency.

In 1968 when the Lutheran Children's Friend Society agreed to merge with Lutheran Social Services (LSS), it was providing services related to adoption, foster care, and counseling for unwed parents and families. In the face of an ever-increasing need, LSS chose to consolidate its adoption-related services in existing LSS facilities and raze the Lutheran Children's Friend Society building. The land was redeveloped for single-family housing in 1975.

Sheltering Arms

In its nearly 75 years in the neighborhood near 44th and West River Parkway, Sheltering Arms has continually adapted to changing conditions to provide social services in demand for the particular time. Serving variously as orphanage, hospital, and school, Sheltering Arms rightly claims the history of three unique neighborhood institutions.

Richard Martin, the banker who acquired some of the land along the river in the 1860s, found little demand for the land and so held onto it until his death in 1890. A lifelong Episcopalian and a physically challenged orphan himself, he donated the land to the church, stipulating its use as an orphanage by some current or future Episcopal group. Martin's executors determined that the Episcopal group Sheltering Arms was eligible to receive the land. Tired of waiting for the land, Sheltering Arms sued the executors and won transfer in 1900.

52 ■ The Neighborhood by the Falls

◀ Sheltering Arms, ca. 1925

Sheltering Arms orphanage in December 1938. The only building still standing is the chapel—the dark-roofed structure to the right of the main building.

Orphanage: 1910–1942

Sister Annette Relf established Sheltering Arms in 1882 to serve disadvantaged and indigent children. Its first orphanage was near downtown Minneapolis, and in 1884 the agency built larger quarters in north Minneapolis. The orphanage quickly became crowded, making clear the need for new quarters. After receiving Martin's donation of land and securities, Sheltering Arms determined that the property near 43rd and West River Parkway was suitable for building a new orphanage. The group had plans drawn up for a two-and-a-half-story brick structure and raised sufficient funds for construction. The new orphanage opened on April 18, 1910, on a 90-acre site stretching from 44th Street on the south to 38th Street on the north and from 46th Avenue east to West River Parkway. The board of directors set aside the 26 acres from 42nd to 44th Streets for the grounds. The sale of remaining land to developers provided the orphanage with an endowment.

In the early 1900s, the government provided few social services. Private, mostly church-run orphanages took care of the children whose families could not. Children stayed at orphanages for extended periods; some, who still had families, eventually reunited with them. That quickly changed with new child welfare laws in the

Social Life ■ 53

In 1920, there were 42 children at the Sheltering Arms orphanage, most between the ages of 5 and 12. The orphanage manager, matron, janitor, cook, five nurses, and three servants all lived on the site with their families. Two years later, in 1922, the agency erected the Church Memorial Chapel—the only orphanage building standing today. For many years it was the scene of weekly worship services, often attended by residents of the larger neighborhood.

Further changes came in the 1930s, when the State of Minnesota began building facilities for the care of indigent children and the new Social Security program provided aid to dependent children. Sheltering Arms adjusted to these changes, adding and dropping programs as needed. During the early years of World War II, its day care center for the children of mothers working in defense plants was one of the first in the neighborhood.

Children in front of Sheltering Arms, ca. 1925. The walls and gateposts still stand today.

Three girls at Sheltering Arms, ca. 1925 ▶

early 1920s establishing the concept of foster homes. Children then stayed at the orphanage a shorter time, as prelude to placement with a family in a foster home. Consequently, many more children came and went through the orphanage in a given year.

When the orphanage opened in 1910, demand was still high, and the board could offer places to just 70 of the 300 children for whom application was made. Those accepted enjoyed amenities provided by the women of the junior board—including gym equipment and even a horse. Vegetable gardens on the grounds supplemented the children's (or inmates, as they were called at the time) diet.

54 ■ The Neighborhood by the Falls

Polio Hospital: 1943–1955

The year 1942 saw a decreasing need for orphanages and an increase in the number of people contracting polio, for which there was then no vaccine. St. Barnabas Hospital (another Episcopal institution) approached the board of Sheltering Arms about creating a recovery home for polio victims released from the hospital.

The now-famous Sister Kenny had developed an innovative technique for treating polio in her native Australia and come to Minneapolis at the request of the Mayo Clinic. The adoption of her successful methods soon made Minneapolis a center for polio treatment, and the demand for treatment facilities was high.

St. Barnabas had adopted the Sister Kenny technique for treating polio and needed a place to provide convalescent care for recovering patients. After much deliberation, the Sheltering Arms board accepted the challenge, closed the orphanage, and applied for a hospital license in May 1942.

> The polio epidemic hit people of all ages, so the new hospital treated a range of patients from young children to older men and women.

It was not to be that easy—the neighborhood wanted its say as well. Residents near the facility circulated a petition against it, and 12th Ward Alderman Norman Irgens held up approval by sending the license back to the Health and Hospitals Committee for a hearing. The committee found no problem with the proposed facility, and the state health commissioner reportedly announced: "There's no danger to the neighborhood whatever." Shortly after the hearing, the license was approved.

Renovation of the property, begun in May, had continued during the controversy. When the fully equipped polio hospital opened early in 1943, it had the capacity to treat 80 (both acute and recovering) patients, and it was the first hospital in the United States exclusively for those with polio. Six men who lived nearby sued in March 1943, shortly after the hospital opened, claiming that it violated zoning laws and would damage property values in the area. They did not prevail.

◀ Polio patient with nurse, c. 1944

The polio epidemic hit people of all ages, so the new hospital treated a range of patients from young children to older men and women. They received Kenny treatments consisting of hot packs and physical therapy, as well as occupational therapy and help with job placement at the end of recovery. Staff members tried to make life as normal as possible for the patients—a teacher provided instruction for school-age children, and there were recreational activities for everyone at 3:30 each day.

Originally licensed for 35 patients, the hospital grew quickly, and at the height of the epidemic in 1952, it had 101. After the development of a polio vaccine in 1955, the epidemic ended. After caring for a total of 2,047 polio patients from across the nation, Sheltering Arms had to reinvent itself again.

Day School for Mentally Retarded Children: 1955–1983

The early 1950s saw increased awareness of and interest in the special needs of mentally challenged children and their parents. Schooling for the younger children existed in most towns, but programs for high-schoolers were nearly nonexistent. Thus, in winter 1954–55, when the Sheltering Arms board asked the Hennepin County Community Welfare Council for advice about what needs its empty hospital might fill, the investigative committee recommended a day school for mentally challenged children. It was to focus on curriculum development, research, and service to families.

Sheltering Arms soon established a partnership with the Minneapolis Public Schools: the district was to provide teachers and a basic school budget; Sheltering Arms, its facilities. The new school opened in fall 1955 with 35 students, ages 6 to 10, in three classrooms.

In the face of great demand for placement in the school, administrators set specific selection criteria so as to bring in students who best fit the needs of the research program. The school gradually grew to accommodate older children, and by 1967 enrollment reached 66 students in six classes. In 1968, the school added a gym and auditorium. Sheltering Arms shared the results of its research and curriculum development with other public schools at conferences and through books and journal articles. Nearby Breck School encouraged its students to volunteer at Sheltering Arms, which also offered practicum placement to University of Minnesota students in a variety of fields. The school served a total of 356 children during its nearly 30 years in operation.

Changing requirements for the education of "special" children plus the increased "mainstreaming" of these children in regular classrooms led to closing the school in the spring of 1983. In September 1982 the Sheltering Arms board voted to sell the property to the Episcopal Church Home for the construction of a 237-unit cooperative apartment complex for people 55 years and older. All the old buildings but the chapel gave way for construction of the new complex—Becketwood.

After the sale of its West River Parkway property, Sheltering Arms continued as a foundation, still seeking to aid vulnerable children and adults with few resources.

The Corner Store

Until the end of the 1950s, scattered small grocery stores served residents across the Longfellow neighborhood—on corners of residential streets and along streetcar lines like 42nd Avenue, Minnehaha Avenue, and Lake Street. These stores offered little selection—mostly they carried dry

3301 31st Avenue, 2007. The Rustads' store, sold in the late 1940s, remained a grocery longer than most. The last store in this building, ironically the "Corner Store," closed in 1975. ▶

3957–59 42nd Avenue, 2007. A grocery and meat market operated here from 1914 until 1956, when the last store, Garden Homes Food Market, closed for good. The meat market operated from the side, and a third storefront occasionally housed a business such a beauty parlor. Somehow the sign on this old corner store has survived for more than 50 years, one of only a few traces left of the old corner stores in Longfellow. ▶

56 ■ The Neighborhood by the Falls

goods like canned goods, flour, soap, and so forth, but they were spaced so that most customers had to walk no more than a block or two. Before automobiles were common, most walked from home or stopped by after getting off the streetcar on the way home from work. Grocers sometimes partnered with the proprietor of a meat market to operate side by side, giving customers more choice and businesses more customers.

The Women's Co-Operative Alliance, a social reform group, had a problem with the corner grocery store. According to its research in the early to mid-1920s, these stores provided an irresistible temptation to area youth with their sweets and other unhealthy foods. Worse yet, the corner store was seen as a "hang-out" for unruly youth and gangs! These loitering places reportedly lured minors with petty (illegal) gambling devices or sold them cigarettes and liquor.

The number of corner stores in the neighborhood peaked in the mid-1930s at nearly 100 total or one for every three blocks. After World War II, the number declined somewhat, but the real drop occurred in the 1950s. At that time larger

◀ Interior, Rustad Grocery, 3301 31st Avenue, 1925. From 1910 to 1949 Norwegian immigrant Arne Rustad and his son Emmet operated this grocery and lived above the store.

◀ Interior, Garden Homes Grocery, 3957–59 42nd Avenue, 1931

Social Life ■ 57

and better-stocked supermarket chains began to pop up in south Minneapolis, catering to the ever-increasing number of households owning a car. By 1960, three quarters of the stores that had existed in 1930 were gone.

One chain, National Tea, had operated in Longfellow since the 1920s. Its small stores appeared, like the corner groceries, across the city. In 1925, National Tea had four stores in Longfellow, and in 1935 it had five. After World War II, when new chains built supermarkets, National Tea joined the trend and closed its smaller stores.

The first supermarket in Longfellow was a National Food Stores (NFS, successor to National Tea) outlet at 38th Street and Dight, built in 1955. Another NFS outlet opened in 1961 near 27th and Lake, where Rainbow Foods now stands. These larger stores, along with those just outside the neighborhood such as the Red Owl at 21st Avenue and Lake Street, caused the demise of the corner grocery store.

By the late 1970s even the NFS outlets were gone, soon to be replaced by the even larger Rainbow Foods (1984) and Cub Foods (1989) stores in the Lake and Minnehaha area. These two stores and a handful of convenience stores dominate the grocery scene today.

Improvement Associations

Improvement associations, the early predecessors of today's neighborhood associations, formed in Longfellow and other parts of the city in the early years of the 20th century. These organizations advocated for improved public services before many basic services had reached the area. In Longfellow, such groups lobbied the Minneapolis City Council for better streets, lighting, new schools, and other city services. As improvements were made, the organizations faded, their reason for existence satisfied. Longfellow was the home of two early improvement associations—Hiawatha and Seven Oaks.

The Hiawatha Improvement Association attracted a lot of attention, including a series of articles in the Minneapolis Journal, *with its new clubhouse.* ▶

Hiawatha Improvement Association

The Hiawatha Improvement Association was the more ambitious of the two, covering the far southern part of Longfellow, generally south of 42nd Street on both sides of Hiawatha Avenue. Organized in May 1908, its members by September had already sold enough stock at $5 a share to secure a lot and commence construction of a clubhouse. Hiawatha Hall, the center of the association's activities at 3725 45th Street, still stands today.

Hiawatha Improvement Association Has Built Its Own Clubhouse

The Hiawatha Improvement association has added another leaf to its wreath of laurel by being the first to erect a permanent home. The manner of its erection was unique. The members of the association contributed the labor, but as many of the members of the organization are busy on week days the clubhouse was built on Sundays. Because of the general interest in the progress of the building and in the purposes of the association the usual objection to the noise of labor on Sunday was waived by the residents of the neighborhood, and the building has gone steadily forward until it is nearly finished. When completed the building, which is at Forty-fifth street and Snelling avenue, will have cost about $3,500. The Hiawatha Improvement association lets nothing interfere with its regular meetings, and at these meetings it has taken effective action on matters pertaining to the welfare of the neighborhood. The social feature is to be elaborated and the clubhouse will have a kitchen for use when the club parties are given.

The founders of the association were average citizens who worked as carpenters, grocers, and electricians. Their purpose was "the improvement and up building of the district, the helping of ones in need, and the general welfare of the community at large, so that anything not desired will certainly not be tolerated by the association."

The association's goals were specific: "Among the important improvements which we have secured might be mentioned—the electric lighting of Forty-second and Forty-fifth streets, hose cart and hose for engine house, cement walks on Forty-second street, better streetcar service on Minnehaha line, eighth grade at Minnehaha school, electric lighting for residence use which will soon be installed, new school building at 45th street and Minnehaha (which will be built this summer), and various other matters which have been done and are continually being brought to the attention of the authorities."

The group successfully lobbied for the first Hiawatha School at 45th and Minnehaha, operating there from 1910 until 1916 when the current Hiawatha School opened at 42nd and 42nd. (The one-story "new" school wasn't totally modern; a 1912 map shows it with boys' and girls' outhouses.)

Over the years, Hiawatha Hall was a venue for concerts, speeches, dances, and other "entertainments," including fundraisers for widows and the sick as well as for the Hiawatha Improvement Association. Such events drew several hundred people, and one fundraiser for the building fund drew more than 400. But dances somehow became controversial before the hall's second birthday: "The dances given at the hall have been respectable at all times, but have been objected to and in the future will be discontinued."

The association, which published a weekly *Improvement Gazetteer* and called on its women's auxiliary to "look after the artistic side" of its work, apparently survived only until about 1914, selling the hall shortly thereafter. The Women's Co-Operative Alliance in 1926 reported neighbors' complaints about the unregulated dances at the renamed R & R Hall. By the early 1930s the hall had become the studio of scenic artist Albert D. Hipp. Since then it has provided studio space and storage.

Seven Oaks Improvement Association

Formed at the same time as the Hiawatha group, the Seven Oaks Improvement Association had similar aims but different origins. Land developer Henry B. Scott of Burlington, Iowa, had invented and first used the "Seven Oaks" marketing name in 1907. Scott was a land agent for railroad baron Charles E. Perkins of Burlington, Iowa, longtime president of the Chicago, Burlington & Quincy Railroad (later Burlington Northern). Scott purchased land on behalf of Perkins, divided it into lots, and worked with local realtor Edmund Walton to market and sell them. Walton started the Seven Oaks Improvement Association so as to improve the area and thus make his lots more valuable, a widespread practice among developers after World War II.

The area in which Perkins's subdivisions were located became known in the early decades of the 20th century as Seven Oaks. Scott, Walton, and later the Seven Oaks Corporation (also associated with Scott) laid out 19 subdivisions with Seven Oaks as part of their names between 1907 and 1925. The original (before 1910) Seven Oaks subdivisions lay between Lake and 34th Streets, 35th to 42nd Avenues but later went all the way to the river and south to 38th Street.

◀ The old Hiawatha Hall at 3725 45th Street, as it appeared in 2008

Soon after Johnson School opened in 1910, storefronts such as that of Seven Oaks Bakery popped up across the street, making the school and its environs the center of the Seven Oaks district. ▶

Seven Oaks Bakery building (at left), 3149 38th Avenue, 2008. Historically, three storefronts in these two buildings housed businesses such as a meat market, a grocery store, and Seven Oaks Bakery. ▶

SEVEN OAKS BAKERY
3151 38th Avenue S.

Established for over two years past, this first class bakery is headquarters for everything in the bakery line, and everything handled is baked right in its own shop, under the personal direction of Mr. A. Heinz, proprietor. A full fresh display is made daily, and you buy nothing old or left over in this place. Confectionery goods are handled also, in nice variety and good quality. Drop in some day and see the shop for yourself. You can't visit it without buying some of the delicious goods made here—you just can't do it, that's all. And a visit will make a regular customer of you, we don't doubt.

The original Seven Oaks subdivision was barely six months old when Edmund Walton presided over the first meeting of the Seven Oaks Improvement Association in April 1908. A hundred "citizens of the district" attended the meeting to choose an executive committee from their midst. Telina Cable, a 63-year-old widow, was elected president; one of Walton's managers, secretary. The balance of the committee consisted of area men of occupations such as carpenter, telegraph operator, and teamster. From the first meeting came the demand: "Better street lighting, a system of sewerage, street crossings, and a schoolhouse." The women at that first meeting were especially excited about the extension of gas mains into the district.

The Seven Oaks Improvement Association did succeed in getting a new school in the district. Johnson School, bounded by 37th and 38th Avenues and by 31st and 32nd Streets, opened in 1910 and served until World War II (the building was demolished and replaced with houses in 1977).

But the association must have faded—local residents, apparently without the instigation of any real estate interests, organized a new Seven Oaks Improvement Association in October 1912. The executive committee of the new organization consisted of residents with occupations like stenographer, carpenter, and grocer. This association, which met at Johnson School, started with more than 200 members. It lasted only a few years, no doubt a victim of its own success.

5 /Entertainment

Entertainment

Sizable venues such as the Wonderland amusement park and the Minnehaha Driving Park drew visitors from across the Twin Cities. The relatively late residential development of Longfellow compared to that in other parts of Minneapolis was the primary reason for venue development in the neighborhood.

Overleaf—
Robert F. Jones feeding sea lions at Longfellow Gardens, c. 1910

Minnehaha Falls was Longfellow's first pleasure-seekers' destination, before Minnesota even became a state. Since then, Longfellow has seen almost every possible large-scale entertainment venue, from movie theater to full-blown amusement park.

Sizable venues such as the Wonderland amusement park and the Minnehaha Driving Park drew visitors from across the Twin Cities. The relatively late residential development of Longfellow compared to that in other parts of Minneapolis was the primary reason for venue development in the neighborhood. As Longfellow grew in population, the

Wonderland Park entrance on Lake Street c. 1907. Wonderland's 120-foot illuminated tower dominated the park with thousands of electric lights topped by spotlights. ▶

62 ■ The Neighborhood by the Falls

◀ Riverview Theater lobby, 1956. The 1950s-era Riverview is the only surviving movie theater in the neighborhood.

Minnehaha Driving Park Association stock certificate, 1888. Shares sold for $50 each.

larger venues gave way to the major entertainment venue of the 20th century—the movie theater.

Longfellow saw its first silent movie theater in 1912, and by the late 1940s there were three "talkie" venues in the neighborhood. The theaters hung on until the 1960s, when competition from television and other entertainment forced two of the three houses to close. Today, only Riverview Theater survives—in 1950s splendor.

Minnehaha Driving Park

In 1888, Robert F. "Fish" Jones raised $50,000 from Minneapolis horseracing enthusiasts to build Minnehaha Driving Park. The one-mile, oval-shaped, racing track sat on 60 acres of land running from 36th to 37th Streets and Minnehaha to 42nd Avenues. The track was for harness racing, which meant that jockeys (drivers) rode in sulkies (two-wheeled carts) pulled by horses, as opposed to riding on saddled horses.

The 1880s were the heyday of harness racing in the Twin Cities. In addition to Minnehaha Driving Park, there were two tracks in St. Paul—the Minnesota State Fair track on Hamline and the Kittsondale track in the Midway district.

No racing took place at Minnehaha Driving Park during the 1888 season as the track was under construction, but trainers did run their drivers and horses there. The multi-purpose track had enough room in the middle for a base-ball diamond as well as a one-third-mile bicycle track.

Entertainment ■ 63

Directum 4, 2:05¼, Harry Hersey up, 1902. Marion Savage of the International Stock Food Company owned Directum 4 and raced at Minnehaha Driving Park in 1895.

During the opening season in 1889, the track hosted two sessions, or meetings, but after that only one meeting occurred yearly, usually around the 4th of July. Each meeting ran from four to seven days with many one-mile or half-mile races, or heats, held each day. Crowds of 6,000 to 7,000 people gathered for many races, packing into the grandstand and along the track to watch and cheer.

Some wealthy spectators traveled to the track with horse and buggy, but the majority of spectators used public transportation. Before the streetcar line extended down Minnehaha Avenue, the only way to get to the track was to take the Motor Line. The Minneapolis, Lyndale and Minnetonka Motor Line traveled along 37th Street from Nicollet Avenue and then on the Hiawatha Avenue railroad tracks to Minnehaha Park. The short-lived Motor Line preceded the electrification of streetcars in the early 1890s, running a small steam engine (locomotive) disguised as a streetcar and towing a passenger car. Beginning in 1891, spectators could take the streetcar down Minnehaha Avenue and get off in front of the park.

Spectators stayed at the track all day, taking in races and other events, such as horse shows, included on some race days. The weather sometimes determined whether a race ran as scheduled. If rain caused the postponement of a race, the crowd waited out the delay; if the track got too muddy, the people simply went home. The year 1895 was a good one for the track; all the horses from the prestigious Grand Circuit raced at the park, and one set a state record. The economic doldrums of the 1890s led the association running the track to declare bankruptcy and close it in 1895.

In an effort to bring the Great Western Trotting Circuit (an association of harness tracks in the Upper Midwest) to Minneapolis, businessmen including Marion Savage and Fish Jones made major renovations to the grounds and buildings in 1901. The effort was successful, and the track reopened for business. The June 8, 1901, season opener featured races and other events: "a regular road riders' parade, with prizes for styles of light, heavy, single, double and four-in-hand rigs, and also liberal offerings for automobile exhibits and rewards for the cyclers." Despite the improvements and increased marketing, the revitalized park was in operation only two years—from 1901 through 1902.

In early 1903 Savage and Jones lost their lease on the property, and the track closed for good. Fish Jones went on to develop Longfellow Gardens at Minnehaha Park in 1907 and to purchase the famous racehorse Dan Patch for Marion Savage.

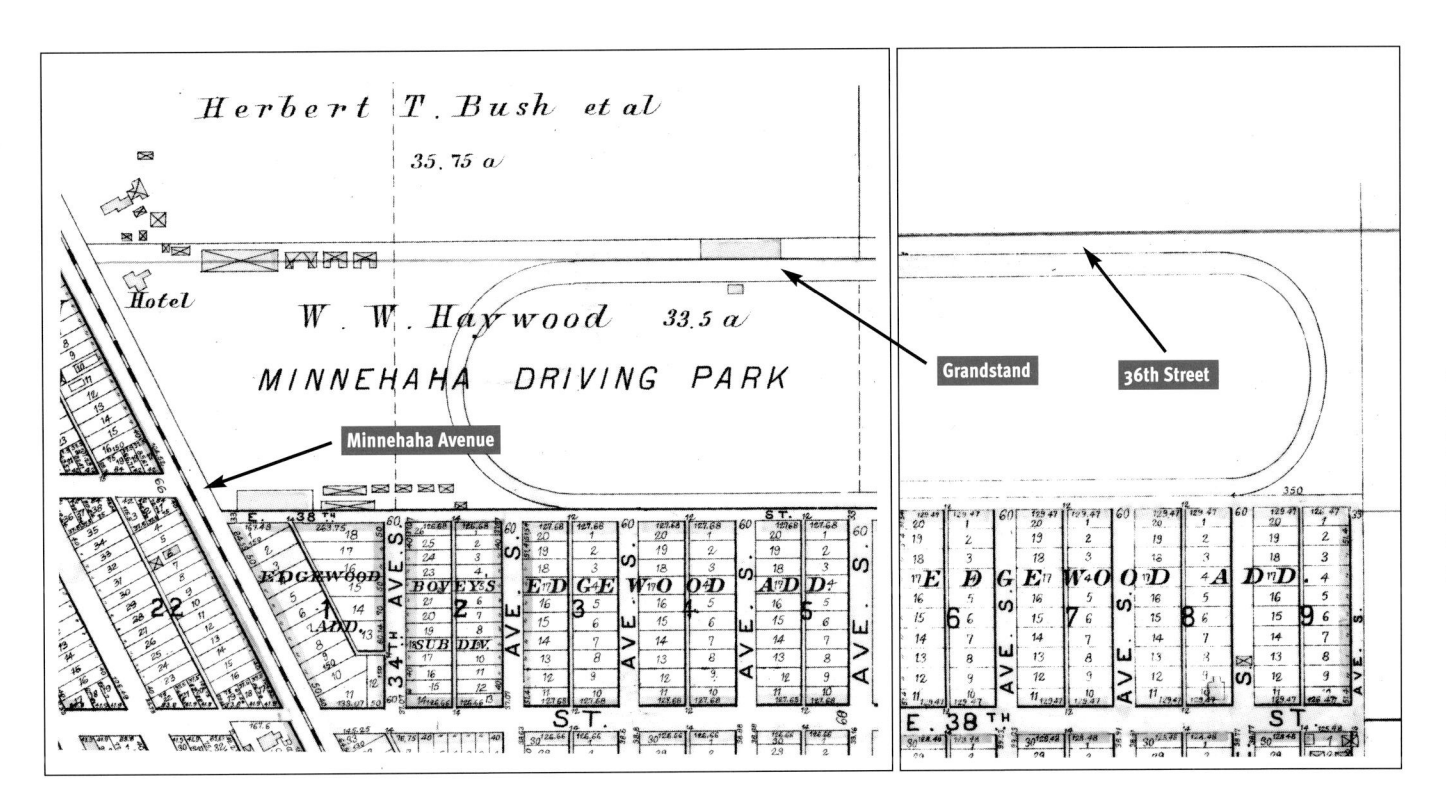

Minnehaha Driving Park and vicinity, 1892. The judges' stand was directly across the track from the grandstand. Note the hotel on Minnehaha Avenue and the stables to its right.

Developers cleared most of the of the buildings of the park shortly after its closing and divided much of the land into lots in 1905. The *Minneapolis Journal* commented in 1903: "Many famous horses have appeared upon the old 'Haha track, and numberless fast miles have been stepped by some of the most famous harness campaigners in the country."

Minneapolis Millers Baseball Team

Even after the Minnehaha Driving Park hosted no races, baseball teams played ball there. The interior of the track accommodated a baseball diamond, and the Minneapolis Millers played Sunday baseball there until 1909. At the turn of the 20th century, many people frowned upon any sort of sport or organized fun on the Sabbath. So on Sundays the Millers left their regular home at Nicollet Park (Nicollet Avenue and Lake Street) to play on the edge of town, where nobody was around to object. In 1909 Sunday baseball became legal, so in 1910 the Millers began to play all their games in Nicollet Park.

Entertainment ■ 65

Minnehaha Park

Minnehaha Falls is arguably Minnesota's oldest tourist attraction and certainly one of its most famous places. Soon after the steamboat *Virginia* first made its way up the Mississippi to Fort Snelling in 1823, tourists began to visit Minnehaha Falls as well as the Falls of St. Anthony. Minnehaha Falls has been the scene of countless photographs, paintings, and weddings since before Minnesota was a state.

> Given its history and its status as a tourist attraction, that **the area around the falls became Minnesota's first state-designated park** is logical.

The name Minnehaha comes from a combination of Dakota words. Mary Eastman, the wife of a Fort Snelling officer and artist, is often credited with coining the name since it appeared in her 1849 book *Dacotah*. On some maps from the early 1800s, the site appeared as "Little Falls," a counterpoint to the larger Falls of St. Anthony. A military map of the time dubbed it "Brown's Falls," probably in honor of U.S. Army commander Jacob Brown, an officer at the time of Fort Snelling's completion.

In 1855 Henry Wadsworth Longfellow used Eastman's "Minnehaha" in his epic poem *The Song of Hiawatha*, giving the falls its lasting name. Oddly, Longfellow never saw the 53-foot waterfall he made famous. For the poem, he drew on a 1851 daguerreotype of the falls and the writings of Henry Rowe Schoolcraft, who had compiled Native American stories of the area. At the end of the fourth section, "Hiawatha and Mudjekeewis," the hero, Hiawatha, decides to go to the land of the Dacotah and woo the beautiful Minnehaha:

Homeward now went Hiawatha;
Pleasant was the landscape round him,
Pleasant was the air above him,
For the bitterness of anger
Had departed wholly from him,
From his brain the thought of vengeance,
From his heart the burning fever.

Only once his pace he slackened,
Only once he paused or halted,
Paused to purchase heads of arrows
Of the ancient Arrow-maker,
In the land of the Dacotahs,
Where the Falls of Minnehaha
Flash and gleam among the oak-trees,
Laugh and leap into the valley.

There the ancient Arrow-maker
Made his arrow-heads of sandstone,
Arrow-heads of chalcedony,
Arrow-heads of flint and jasper,
Smoothed and sharpened at the edges,
Hard and polished, keen and costly.

With him dwelt his dark-eyed daughter,
Wayward as the Minnehaha,
With her moods of shade and sunshine,
Eyes that smiled and frowned alternate,
Feet as rapid as the river,
Tresses flowing like the water,
And as musical a laughter;
And he named her from the river,
From the water-fall he named her,
Minnehaha, Laughing Water.

Was it then for heads of arrows,
Arrow-heads of chalcedony,
Arrow-heads of flint and jasper,
That my Hiawatha halted
In the land of the Dacotahs?

Was it not to see the maiden,
See the face of Laughing Water
Peeping from behind the curtain,
Hear the rustling of her garments
From behind the waving curtain,
As one sees the Minnehaha
Gleaming, glancing through the branches,
As one hears the Laughing Water
From behind its screen of branches?

Who shall say what thoughts and visions
Fill the fiery brains of young men?
Who shall say what dreams of beauty
Filled the heart of Hiawatha?
All he told to old Nokomis,
When he reached the lodge at sunset,
Was the meeting with his father,
Was his fight with Mudjekeewis;
Not a word he said of arrows,
Not a word of Laughing Water.

Given its history and its status as a tourist attraction, that the area around the falls became Minnesota's first state-designated park is logical. In 1885, the Minnesota Legislature voted to establish such a park at Minnehaha Falls. The state lent the City of Minneapolis the money necessary to buy the 120-acre site from a private owner, which it did officially in 1889. The Minneapolis Board of Park Commissioners later expanded the park to 193 acres.

For nearly 200 years regular folk and dignitaries such as Henry David Thoreau, Mark Twain (Samuel L. Clemens), and President Lyndon B. Johnson visited the falls. Hikers can stand in Johnson's "footprints" near the falls today and read how the city ensured the president a memorable experience.

Between 1907 and 1934, Fish Jones, the colorful entrepreneur behind Minnehaha Driving Park, operated a zoo and ornamental garden called Longfellow Gardens adjacent to Minnehaha Park. Visitors arrived at the park by streetcar or train and walked west to the entrance. A prominent feature of the zoo was its aviaries. Exotic birds roamed next to a big cage featuring cranes, herons, swans, ducks, and more. The sea-lion rookery was a popular spot at which Jones often appeared in a top hat and Prince Albert coat to feed the trained animals.

Deer and elk mingled in a pen area below the falls. In other parts of the zoo, caged lions, bears, jungle cats, elephants, camels, buffalo, and Tasmanian devils were on display. Concerts, a miniature railway, animal shows, and an amphitheater with seating for a thousand added to the hustle and bustle. Patrons got the full value of their 15-cent admission!

Picnickers at Minnehaha Park, c. 1905

Entertainment 67

As the neighborhood expanded towards the zoo, however, nearby residents began to complain about the noise and smell. The city condemned it in the early 1920s, but Jones persuaded officials to let him keep the zoo there until he died. After Jones's death in 1930, his daughter ran the zoo another four years before turning the land over to the city. A concessionaire ran the pony ring there until the late 1940s.

Fish Jones built a two-thirds-size reproduction of Longfellow's Cambridge, Massachusetts, home adjacent to Longfellow Gardens in 1923. It replicated many features of the original Longfellow house, including a dumbwaiter to bring food upstairs from the basement kitchen, a clock on the stairs, and an oval mirror over the fireplace. Reproduction furniture occupied the same spots as the originals in the eastern house. Jones and his family lived in the house until 1934. Later the Minneapolis Library Board opened the house as a library. Moved from the west side of Hiawatha Avenue to its current location in 1994 as part of the rerouting and rebuilding of Hiawatha Avenue, the house now serves as office space and information center for the Minneapolis Park and Recreation Board.

Minnehaha Park retains other traces of the past. The whimsical Princess Depot, built in the mid-1870s, once served as many as 39 daily trains, bringing visitors to the park and soldiers to Fort Snelling. Crews organized by the Works Progress Administration (WPA) in the late 1930s built many of the park's retaining walls and steps still in use today. The quarry used by the workers is no longer visible, but traces are evident near the smokestack of the former garbage incinerator at the park's southern end.

A tourist camp flourished from 1922 to 1955 in what is now the Waubun Picnic Area. The camp drew hundreds of tent and car campers. For those interested in a less rustic experience, log cabins were available. After the WPA constructed 10 cabins in 1936 the camp had a total of 36 cabins for the 7,000-plus annual visitors. Campers paid 50 cents a night, an additional 10 cents for electricity. The Minneapolis Park Board typically earned $10,000 per year from the tourist camp—not bad for a depression-era business!

In 1992 the Minneapolis Park and Recreation Board completed a master plan for improvements to the park. In 1994 the park underwent alterations associated with the realignment of Hiawatha Avenue (Minnesota Highway 55). A land bridge at the northwest corner replaced the land taken for the realignment at the south end of the park. The land bridge covers the highway, effectively connecting Longfellow House with Minnehaha Creek. In the area of the historical Longfellow Gardens, a new public garden now graces the land bridge. Plans are underway to control erosion and stabilize the WPA-built walls lining the creek below the falls.

Family at Minnehaha Park tourist camp, 1925

Wonderland Park

In the transition between a rural and residential Longfellow, the neighborhood had its own big amusement park. From 1905 to 1911, Wonderland Park was a major summer attraction, open from late May to early September. It was roughly six square blocks (10 acres), from 31st to 33rd Avenues and Lake to 32nd Streets. H. A. Dorsey of Montreal, Quebec, Canada, developed this park along with similar amusement parks in Chicago and Milwaukee. Chicago's White City, Wonderland Park Milwaukee, and Wonderland Park Minneapolis opened simultaneously on May 27, 1905. Citizens of the Twin Cities purchased $150,000 in stock to finance the venture. The Lake Street streetcar line stretched to Wonderland just in time for the opening.

Wonderland dominated the landscape with its 120-foot electrically lighted tower serving as the focal point for stunts, aerial acts, and even a wedding. The tower had a spotlight on top, giving it the appearance of a lighthouse on the prairie of south Minneapolis. At its peak, Wonderland had 30 buildings and 32 substantial flowerbeds. The park could accommodate 50,000 visitors a day, and more than 70,000 went through the gates on opening day, paying 5 cents each for children and 10 cents for adults. A 12-foot-high solid-wood fence surrounded the park to keep out those wanting to get in for free.

Wonderland was all about escape from everyday life to exotic and exciting places and times. Patrons bought their tickets at the gates from women cashiers in Mexican dress. Attendants for the "Shooting the Chutes" boat ride dressed in sailor uniforms. A person could travel to exotic places—like Chilkoot Pass, associated with the Klondike Gold Rush—ride the scenic railway (rollercoaster), and view exhibits such as one on the Johnstown Flood.

Wonderland's attractions were typical for amusement parks of the day, but its proprietors, who insisted on displaying only genuine exhibits, reportedly had higher standards than those of some East Coast parks. Generally the park did not offend morality crusaders of the time. The Rev. G. L. Morrill, a visiting clergyman, had these words of praise: "The people are listening to good music and indulging in innocent and healthful sport. There is nothing loud or tough here; in fact this park is an example of good order that other amusement resorts should pattern after."

To avoid the potential improprieties of darkened vaudeville halls or auditoriums, the park featured an enclosed theater stage viewed by spectators through lenses magnifying the scenes inside. The Wonderland Fairy Theater performed plays, particularly fairy tales like *Jack and the Bean-stalk*, in pantomime.

The only controversy occurred just after the park opened. In 1905 the Elim Presbyterian Church was just across Lake Street from the new amusement park at the northwest corner of 32nd and Lake. Church members were unhappy that the park would be open on Sundays and claimed that its lights and noise would rule out evening services. The church sued Wonderland Park, and the parties even-

Bumping the Bumps, an attraction at which visitors rolled down a padded incline

tually settled. Wonderland bought lots nearby and paid for moving the church to the northeast corner of 30th Avenue and 33rd Street. The congregation later renamed it the Vanderburgh Presbyterian Church. Indian Fellowship Church now occupies that building.

Attractions

Wonderland Park had rides, funhouses, exhibits, an electric theater, daredevil performances, a fortuneteller, a penny arcade, and daily fireworks, among other attractions. New traveling acts came through often. In 1911 "Aeroplane Ladies" hung "by their teeth to wires attached to a flying machine anchored high in the air. They have the appearance of flying and the spectacle is a pretty one." The park had its own electric-power substation, as it was on the edge of the city and electricity was still relatively rare.

The rollercoaster was known as a "scenic railway," not only giving riders thrills and chills as it zoomed up and down but also taking them on a tour of exotic places. In the hype leading to the opening of Wonderland in late May 1905, the *Minneapolis Journal* reported:

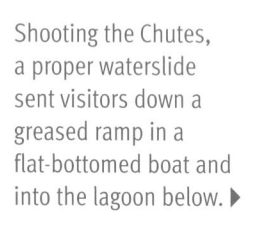

House of Nonsense, one of three funhouses at Wonderland Park, offered a series of practical jokes. ▶

Shooting the Chutes, a proper waterslide sent visitors down a greased ramp in a flat-bottomed boat and into the lagoon below. ▶

◀ Looking northeast from the top of Shooting the Chutes towards Lake Street in the distance. At the top is the scenic railway (roller-coaster); at lower left are two cars of the Wonderland Limited miniature railway.

North end of the scenic railway
▼

The scenic railway affords an exhilaration enjoyed by all. The descent is made with great swiftness down a declivity, then up again to a height equal to that from which the start was made, fifty feet from the ground. Next, a plunge into a dark tunnel, then a whirl around the loop and a trip along the bank of a river past the ruins of an old church, another tunnel and a dip into the Devil's cave. Then into the open air and another descent, a steep plunge downward down a toboggan, which sends you kiting up again and around a sharp curve into a deep mountain ravine, where you see a volcano in eruption, and then glide smoothly along the shore with a view of ocean expanse, and the journey is ended. The trip has taken only a few minutes, but it has seemed much longer.

Entertainment ■ 71

Infant Incubator

One of Wonderland's most unusual features was its hospital for premature babies—the Infant Incubator Institute. On what is now the southeast corner of 31st Street and 31st Avenue, the hospital had two stories.

Incubators for premature infants first appeared in the United States in 1898 and quickly became an attraction at amusement parks across the nation. Hospitals were reluctant to buy the expensive machines, so the doctors who developed them turned to amusement parks as a way to publicize the technology and garner popular support. Hospitals had been able to do little for premature infants, only about 15 percent of whom survived if the parents could afford hospital treatment at all. The incubator technology, said to save more than three-fourths of the infants it treated, created a carefully controlled environment, providing much greater chances for infant survival.

Before-and-after shots of premature infants treated in the Wonderland Park incubators ▶

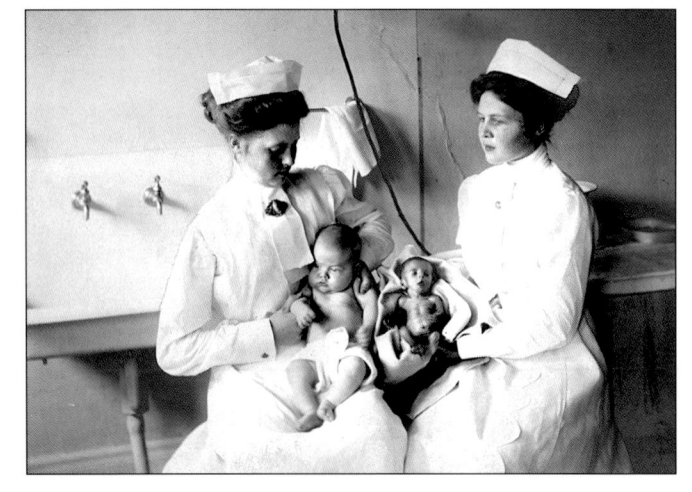

The incubator hospitals were unique in charging parents nothing for treating their infants and in its lack of discrimination based on income, race, and so forth. The small fee charged visitors to the Infant Incubator Institute was enough to cover the cost of hospital staff and equipment. The Infant Incubator Institute reportedly was the main attraction at Wonderland.

The End of Wonderland

The year 1911 was Wonderland Park's last; in April 1912 it was dismantled. Several factors contributed to its demise: the 1911 season was cold and wet, and attendance was low; Lake Street had been paved in 1909, raising assessments including those for the park; and some of the rides and equipment were wearing down and had been condemned. Urban legend has it that many of the boards salvaged from the amusement park became part of the new houses built nearby. Today, all that remains of Wonderland is the much-altered Infant Incubator Institute building, now an apartment building at 3101–11 East 31st Street.

Movie Theaters

Movie theaters got their start from the live stage. The Pence Opera House in downtown Minneapolis opened in 1867, followed by others such as the Shubert Theatre in 1910. Vaudeville entertainment was popular in the 1870s and 1880s, as were variety show venues in the 1880s and 1890s. Some featured roller-skating monkeys! In the 1920s, moving pictures became the rage, and many former stage theaters became movie theaters. The Orpheum in downtown Minneapolis was one of these. There was no shortage of movie theaters in south Minneapolis. The East Lake, Elite, Nokomis, Rialto, and Rosebud movie theaters thrived on Lake Street and in other areas close to Longfellow.

Longfellow's First Theaters

The first movie theaters in Longfellow were in the 27th and Lake area. The earliest neighborhood theater was the Elk Theater at 2707 East Lake Street in the newly constructed Oddfellows Building. This theater operated from about 1912 to 1917. It was a long, narrow venue, so small the projector had to run from 13 feet outside the theater in an adjacent lot. Its short life and ultimate demise were

Nine Years of New-Found Profits

The Lake Amusement Company in their letter stress the fact that they have time-tested the Butter-Kist proposition, and have found satisfactory profits over a period of nine years. No wonder they add Butter-Kist equipment in each new theatre they build.

The Butter-Kist machine is built to endure, and to produce these unusual profits year in and year out. Hundreds of theatre owners and managers point with pride to the records of our older models installed years ago. We are proud of these records. Hundreds will this year install the new models. Will you be one?

Lake Theatre, c. 1920s, as shown in a Butter-Kist Company promotional brochure

likely due to the opening in 1915 of the much larger Lake Theatre at 2721 East Lake Street.

Lake Theatre

The Lake Theatre, built in 1915, had 698 seats and was one of four theaters owned by the Lake Amusement Company. This group of theaters, like many of the time, obtained films through a "block system" by which several films were provided to the group rather than by each theater choosing individual films.

This system was of great concern to a group of civic-minded women studying the community conditions of south Minneapolis in 1926. At the same time the Butter-Kist Company was trying to promote its new popcorn machines, the Women's Co-Operative Alliance was rating movie theaters on cleanliness, lighting, supervision, and familiarity between boys and girls at the theaters. The alliance judged Lake Theatre to have good lighting but poor sanitation, ventilation, and music. No supervision was observed although a curfew notice appeared on the screen. The alliance also said that the decoration was "overdone," that the children there were disorderly, and that an amateur vaudeville act had included a "very young child performing." At least there were no gangs around the corner, as was the case with both the Minnehaha Theater at Minnehaha and 40th Street and the Elite Theater at 25th Street and 27th Avenue.

The Lake Theatre survived until the early 1960s when Holy Trinity Church acquired the building and land as part of its large-scale urban renewal plan. The theater was demolished in 1964, and the Minneapolis Public Library bought the land in the early 1970s for a new East Lake Library, opening in 1976. In 2007, a substantially remodeled East Lake Library reopened on the site.

El Lago Theatre

The El Lago Theatre opened at 3506 Lake Street in 1927 during the transition from silent films to talkies. It had an orchestra pit for live musicians accompanying silent films, but the quick adoption of films with talking actors and recorded music soon made the pit obsolete. The Lake Amusement Company, El Lago's owner and operator, also built the Lake Theatre and others along Lake Street. El Lago was the farthest east of at least eight movie theaters lining Lake Street from Hennepin to the Mississippi River.

With exotic facade and Spanish name (El Lago means "The Lake"), the theater was all about fantasy and escape from the everyday world. Some described the

Old El Lago Theatre, 2009. Storefronts flanked the left side of the showhouse. ▶

Lake Amusement Company letterhead, 1926. This company built both the El Lago and Lake Theatres. ▶

difficult-to-categorize building as "a 1920s interpretation of 16th-century Italian, with a Georgian, almost Baroque facade." Located a block from the intersection of two streetcar lines, its easily drew moviegoers from Longfellow and surrounding neighborhoods. While prosperous in its early years, El Lago met its demise in 1966 due to the dismantling of the streetcar network in 1954 and the increasing popularity of television. After sitting vacant for several years, it housed a television dealership from 1970 to 1980. The Abundant Life Christian Center moved into the building in 1982; the Victory Christian Center has since taken its place.

Falls Theater

Operating under at least four different names, this 300-seat theater opened at 3950 Minnehaha in 1917. The Falls Theater (its final name before closing) was similar in size and layout to Longfellow's first movie theater, the Elk. The Falls was the Minnehaha Theater in 1926, when the Women's Co-operative Alliance set its sights on such establishments in south Minneapolis.

The alliance was concerned with movie theaters since so many of the audience were impressionable children needing close supervision. It rated each theater on several

Falls Theatre Has Phoney Union Sign

"Believe it or Not" Ripley or "Strange as it May Seem" Hix should be able to make something out of the peculiar antics of a few scabs who have brought out a new racketeering scheme under the name of the "Independent Moving Picture Operators Union, Inc." This small clique sought to end the depression by offering their "services" to the movie houses of Minneapolis for approximately one-half the salary paid the legitimate union oerators who are members of Local 219, I. A. T. S. E. & M. P. M. O. Knowing the calibre of the men, the movie managers wisely rejected the offer and continued employing members of the 'bona fide union. The racketeers retaliated by placing "unfair" banners in front of two south town union houses hoping to drive a little business into the one theatre where they have a man working.

This theatre, the Falls, located at 40th and Minnehaha, seeks to fool the theatre goers with a fake Union Operator sign displayed in front, but the "unfair" banner carried by Local 219 is seen and understood by the former patrons of this theatre. Ripley and Hix may be able to figure it out, but real union men and women will have a hard time understanding how a business can be "unfair" to a couple of racketeers by employing American Federation of Labor Union men and paying nearly double the wages asked by the pretenders.

◀ Article from the *Minneapolis Labor Review* on the union controversy at the Falls Theatre, 1932

aspects, giving the Minnehaha Theater a low score. It was dark and had poor lighting and ventilation but fair music. Alarmingly, children comprised more than three-fourths of its audience while the theater did nothing to enforce the 9 p.m. city curfew other than to flash a clock on the screen. Even more distressing were these findings: "Decoration gaudy. Wall aisle so narrow people obliged to walk sideways. Gang around corner outside." The Minnehaha didn't sound like a good place for any child.

The venue gained further notoriety during the labor unrest of the 1930s. Many theaters had unionized operators in the early 1930s, but the Falls Theater wasn't one of them. Apparently in about 1932, the theater's management wanted to attract customers loyal to union shops while paying sub-union wages. The management formed a fake union—Independent Moving Picture Operators Union, Inc.—to obtain union credibility. The fake union apparently did not attract the attention of other theater owners, so it must have been short-lived. A photo dated February 18, 1932, in the collections of the Minnesota Historical Society, indicates some violence, however. Its caption reads: "Stores adjoining the Falls Theater, 3954 Minnehaha Avenue, damaged by a bomb intended for the theater, Minneapolis."

The theater appears to have had an uneventful run during the rest of the 1930s and the 1940s. It closed in 1948 when its owners, Sidney and William Volk, opened a new theater, the Riverview, at 42nd Avenue and 38th Street. The Falls Theater building still stands at 3950 Minnehaha, currently in use as an office building.

Riverview Theater

The 800-seat Riverview Theater opened at 3800 42nd Avenue on December 30, 1948, as a replacement for the small, aging Falls Theater. The owners of both theaters were brothers Sidney and William Volk, who also owned three others in Minneapolis and one in Robbinsdale. The premier theater architecture firm of Liebenberg and Kaplan was the original architect of Riverview, and this firm did the 1956 remodel as well.

Riverview was modern in every sense of the word from its décor to the layout of the lobby. The design of the spacious lobby and lounge eliminated many of the walls and rooms that made older theater lobbies "boxy," providing for half-walls or partitions instead. The opening of Riverview coincided with the high point of American cinema. In 1948, there were more movie theaters in America than at any other time, releasing a record number of films that year. The first show at Riverview was *June Bride*, starring Bette Davis and Robert Montgomery.

Barely seven years after it opened, Riverview was updated in 1956 with ultra-modern décor featuring unusual wood paneling, imported lamps, Italian tile, and a two-level

Entertainment ■ 75

Riverview Theater, 2009 ▶

Riverview Theater lobby, 1956. At center right (behind the railing) is the famous drinking fountain "mysteriously suspended in space." ▶

copper drinking fountain. The owners gave the architects carte blanche and told them to spare no expense. Many area theaters of the time invested large sums in lobby makeovers, showing they were "supremely confident of theatres' ability to weather the TV storm" and apparently "unafraid of the big bad TV wolf." The owners felt the most attractive, luxurious, and modern theaters had the best chance of competing with TV and other forces working against their success.

Riverview has always been a second-run theater, showing movies only after other theaters have released them. Offering movies for a fraction of what first-run theaters charge doesn't seem likely to go out of fashion soon, and the practice has probably contributed to Riverview's success. In 1999 the theater was outfitted with new high-backed seats with more leg room. Stadium seating, though the new megaplexes advertise it as a new concept, has been part of the Riverview from the start. Despite the closing of nearly all the other neighborhood theaters, Riverview, with its luxurious 1950s décor, has prospered.

6/Building Longfellow

Building Longfellow

In less than 30 years, Longfellow went from a semi-rural area on the edge of the city to the neighborhood it is today. It developed all the features of a medium sized town—a downtown (27th and Lake), industry, and block after block of modest homes.

In the first two-and-a-half decades of the 20th century, Longfellow went from a sleepy township dominated by dairy farms to a bustling community of industry and vibrant commercial and residential districts. Between 1905 and 1929, nearly 80 percent of the present housing stock appeared along with commercial districts at 27th and Lake, along Lake Street and Minnehaha Avenue, and in neighborhood commercial nodes along the streetcar lines. Residential development followed the establishment of each of the three streetcar lines in the neighborhood.

Overleaf and at right—Westbound Selby-Lake streetcar at Minnehaha, c. 1925. The men boarding the streetcar probably worked at Minneapolis Steel and Machinery, the large brick building behind the streetcar. ▶

As in much of the nation, Longfellow experienced a building boom in the 1920s. In the years between 1920 and 1929, the number of houses doubled, and commercial enterprises spread from "downtown Longfellow" at 27th and Lake through the neighborhood. The automobile came of age in the 1920s, and many businesses popped up along Lake Street to service the increasingly ubiquitous auto. Additional schools served the booming areas closer to the Mississippi River and in the southern part of the neighborhood.

The addition of railroad tracks on the western edge of the neighborhood in the 1860s made it a prime spot for the development of industry. Building on Minneapolis's preeminent position in American milling, early industry in Longfellow reflected both agriculture and the grain trade. The northwest corner of Minnehaha Avenue and Lake Street was the site of several farm-implement manufacturers, starting in 1872 with the Minneapolis Harvester Works and ending with Minneapolis-Moline, which closed in 1973. From the late 1880s, grain elevators operated along the railroad tracks. Grain mills followed in 1915, as the milling industry gradually moved from the Falls of St. Anthony.

Infrastructure

Until about 1910, residential areas in Longfellow had few of the modern amenities considered essential today. Water, sewer, electricity, and telephone service were nonexistent, or available in only a few areas, north of 27th and Lake. The practice of building houses first and providing utilities later hung on until the 1910s. The land remained untouched until such time as lots were sold and houses built. After that, streets were graded. Sidewalks might be put in with each house or installed when there were houses enough to do a block. Utilities such as water and sewer came later.

Water and Sewer

A few streets in the area north of 27th and Lake Street had water service before 1900, but not until 1908 did any streets enjoy sewer service. Even the presence of water or sewer pipes did not guarantee any particular home's connection, as homeowners often could decide whether or not to connect to them. Not until 1910 did Minneapolis see a widespread sewer-and-water system or treat its water. Progressive reforms at that time led to the expansion of the city sewer system and the creation of a drinking-water treatment system.

Since clean water was a higher public-health priority, water service tended to become available before sewer service. Diseases like dysentery, caused by contaminated water, were a big problem in the first years of the 20th century. The proximity of wells and outhouses in urban areas engendered the contamination of drinking water, and city delivery of clean, disease-free water could halt the spread of disease even with outhouses still in use.

Extending the 38th Street sewer main, near the Mississippi River, 1909

Looking north on Minnehaha from 37th Street, c. 1910 ▶

In 1909, water service in Longfellow prevailed mostly in the areas north of Lake Street, but by 1913 it had increased dramatically, reaching to most built-up areas.

In 1909, a sewer main installed along 38th Street to the Mississippi River carried untreated sewage to the river. This allowed the expansion of sewer service south of Lake Street, though by 1913 sewer service still was spotty. Subdivisions established after 1905 generally had sewer and water service put in at the time of subdivision, with homes hooked up before the first owners moved in. In older subdivisions, the service was sporadic, and some time passed before all of Longfellow's houses could claim hookups to both water and sewer service.

Paving

The city paved major streets like Minnehaha Avenue and Lake Street early, but residential streets remained unpaved during much of the 20th century. Lake Street was paved to the Mississippi in 1909; Minnehaha Avenue, in about 1920. Residential streets of gravel or oiled dirt prevailed until 1961, when Minneapolis undertook a 30-year residential paving program, paving different parts of its residential streets with cement, and later asphalt, each year.

The first area paved under the program was the Luella A. Anderson Addition in Longfellow, between 46th Avenue and Edmund Boulevard, 40th and 42nd Streets. This was a new subdivision and an easy place to start. The type of paving, cement or asphalt, varies and doesn't follow a set pattern. The earliest areas to be paved, such as the northwest corner of the neighborhood west of 36th Avenue, have streets paved in cement. Later, the preferred material was asphalt which was used for the remaining areas such as east of 36th Avenue around Lake Street. Even as late as 1983, the city was paving some streets in Longfellow for the first time. The program ended up taking 36 years, with the paving of the city's last residential street in 1997.

Streetcars

The streetcar, or electric railway, was the primary method of local travel for Longfellow residents until after World War II. Before widespread use of the automobile, the streetcar was the only quick and reliable way for most people to get to work, entertainment venues, or anyplace else beyond walking distance.

Unlike public transportation today, the streetcar system was privately owned. The Twin City Rapid Transit Company (TCRT) operated one of the most extensive and high-quality streetcar systems in the United States from 1891 until 1954, when it dismantled in favor of buses. Besides running a profitable business, the businessmen who founded TCRT invested in real estate along the line, profiting handsomely when the easy access to transportation increased property values. Streetcar service was a necessary precedent to extensive residential development.

Streetcar service in Longfellow began in 1886 with extension of the horse-car line a few blocks down 27th Avenue to Lake Street, where it terminated. A team of two horse horses slowly pulled a small streetcar on the line. In 1891 the electrified Minnehaha Falls–Fort Snelling line reached farther down Minnehaha Avenue, from where the old horse-pulled line ended at 27th and Lake, to Minnehaha Park.

The new streetcar line made possible the development of areas along Minnehaha. Although few houses rose before the Panic of 1893, the area within one or two blocks of Minnehaha saw construction earlier than that even one or two blocks farther from the line. From 1900 to 1905, nearly all the houses built in the neighborhood were

Looking west along 34th Street towards 37th Avenue, Longfellow Park at left, 1958. Even in the late 1950s, residential streets such as 34th were still of oiled dirt.

Building Longfellow ■ 81

Southbound Minnehaha Falls–Fort Snelling streetcar on Minnehaha at 44th Street, c. 1950. Note the "Car Stop" sign on the utility pole at upper left. ▶

close to Minnehaha. Today, the No. 7 Metro Transit bus runs down Minnehaha Avenue, its service reduced after installation of the nearby Hiawatha Light Rail Line.

Tracks for the streetcar on Lake Street, the Selby-Lake line, were laid across south Minneapolis to 31st Avenue in 1905 in time for the opening of Wonderland Park. A year later it reached all the way down Lake Street and over the Lake Street Bridge to St. Paul. Again, the extension of the streetcar opened an area for development, and home building picked up on the remaining land along Lake Street starting in 1907. Selby-Lake became one of the busiest lines in the system, with service running every three minutes during peak hours, every seven minutes off peak. Today, the No. 21 Metro Transit bus runs along what is still one of the busiest routes of the city.

The final streetcar line in the neighborhood, the East 25th Street line, served the interior and eastern parts of the neighborhood. Extended through most of the neighborhood in 1921, it followed a zigzag route to minimize walking distance for its riders. It ran along 36th Avenue to 34th Street, along 34th Street to 42nd Avenue, then along 42nd Avenue to 41st Street and along 41st Street to 46th Avenue, where it terminated. In 1927, the line stretched over the new Ford Bridge to the Ford plant in St. Paul.

The line stimulated the development of residential areas in the eastern and southern parts of Longfellow, and many small businesses opened along the way. Today, the No. 24 Metro Transit bus follows the same route as the East 25th Street line except that it terminates at the 46th Street Hiawatha Light Rail station.

82 ■ The Neighborhood by the Falls

◀ Eastbound Selby-Lake streetcar at 36th and Lake, c. 1951. Note part of the El Lago Theatre sign above the streetcar.

Housing Development

Signs showing the way into Longfellow announce it as a "Traditional Bungalow Community" for its many small bungalows. Small, simple, yet practical homes such as bungalows are the mainstay of Longfellow's housing stock. Regardless of vintage, nearly all homes in Longfellow are modest in size and stature, indicative of the working-class people who built and lived in them. While any particular street is likely to have like-sized homes, the variety in age and style is striking. Fifty or more years often separate the oldest and newest houses on a given block.

In Longfellow, the survey and platting of land into lots and the creation of subdivisions preceded home construction. Dorilus Morrison platted the first subdivision in 1873, long before anyone dreamed of building houses so far from the small town of Minneapolis. The booming 1880s saw the platting of large subdivisions, mainly north of Lake Street and on both sides of Minnehaha Avenue. Even then, people considered the area to be on the far edge of the city, and it was still mostly farmland. If the building boom of the 1880s and early 1890s had continued, new homes might have filled those lots, but the Panic of 1893 put a stop to new construction.

The ensuing economic depression lasted the better part of 10 years, and little in the way of home building or subdivision occurred in Longfellow—or in the rest of the city. The economy began to improve in about 1905, and with the opening of the Minneapolis Steel and Machinery plant at Lake and Minnehaha, the demand for housing grew.

Walton's Home Builder, June 1915. Walton's Fifth Division was the only Seven Oaks subdivision north of Lake Street—between Lake and 28th Streets, 34th and 36th Avenues. ▶

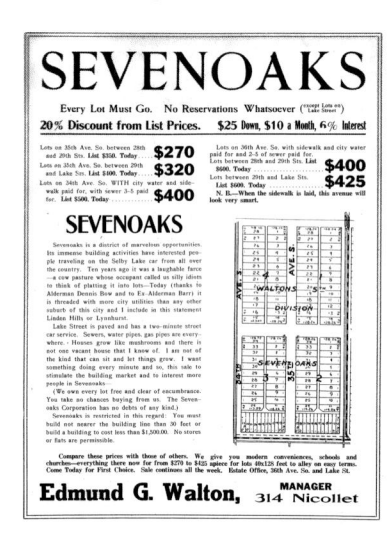

The Walton Agency published a magazine promoting its subdivisions and homes. The style of home held by the builder (dubbed "cottage") was common in Longfellow from about 1907 to 1915, after which the bungalow dominated. ▶

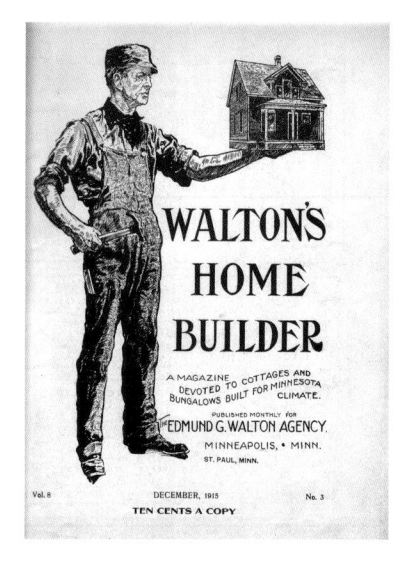

As the old subdivisions filled up with new houses, more lots were platted to the east and south. Home construction picked up in 1908, clipping along at a steady pace through 1919. By the end of that year, about 40 percent of the homes in Longfellow were in place. By the early 1920s the vast majority of the land had been divided into building lots.

The 1920s saw a huge jump in home construction. In that decade alone, another nearly 40 percent of Longfellow's current housing stock came into being. During that time, the bungalow style of home predominated. One-and-a-half-story bungalows filled in the blocks around the neighborhood. The bungalow boom peaked in 1925 and slowly declined before the 1929 stock market crash and subsequent economic depression. After World War II, modest ramblers filled most of the remaining scattered vacant lots, but the new building activity was minimal in comparison to the 1920s boom.

Seven Oaks

During the housing boom of 1908 to 1929, small builders predominated, constructing most homes from standard plans or, in some cases, kits. A notable exception was the Walton Agency, which first used modern real-estate-development practices. In the Seven Oaks subdivisions, the Edmund G. Walton Agency sold land but also provided everything that new homeowners needed. Walton sold the buyer a lot, provided a catalog of house plans, financed the house and lot, and provided the builder. Such one-stop shopping for a new home is commonplace today, but at the turn of the 20th century, it was much less common.

Walton was an early adopter of covenants restricting building types and setting minimum construction costs. These inflated the price of the lots, required larger homes on the lots, and so discouraged pay-as-you-go homeowners, whose small and potentially substandard houses might lower property values. A Seven Oaks ad, above right, instructed: "Sevenoaks [*sic*] is restricted in this regard: You must build not nearer the building line than 30 feet or build a building to cost less than $1,500.00. No stores or flats are permissible." Walton was also ahead of his time in installing sewer lines before home construction.

Land agent Henry B. Scott of Burlington, Iowa, had invented the name "Seven Oaks," for subdivisions platted on behalf of Charles E. Perkins of the Chicago, Burlington & Quincy Railroad. (See chapter 4, page 59). Scott, Walton, and later the Seven Oaks Corporation laid out 19 Seven Oaks subdivisions in Longfellow between 1907 and 1925. The Seven Oaks subdivisions took up a good portion of the northeast corner of the neighborhood, south of Lake Street to 37th Street and east of 35th Avenue. In his advertisements, Walton bragged about the transformation of the area: "Ten years ago it was a laughable farce—a cow pasture whose occupant called us silly idiots to think of platting it into lots." Scott also platted other subdivisions, most along the Mississippi River.

84 ■ The Neighborhood by the Falls

Housing Styles

Longfellow is notable for its lack of large homes of readily discernible style. Working-class people, able to afford only small homes with little ornamentation, settled the neighborhood. The simple homes go by the name of cottage, bungalow, or rambler, according to the specific era of construction. The only exception is the group of larger homes near West River Parkway, generally east of 46th Avenue. Built from the late 1920s to World War II, they are of the eclectic styles common in middle-class homes of the period.

Also of note is a small area of homes of modern style in the Luella A. Anderson Addition between 40th and 42nd Street, 46th Avenue and Edmund Boulevard. The variety of 1960s and 1970s styles in this subdivision includes International, Shed, and a naturalistic style reminiscent of Frank Lloyd Wright.

Housing built in the neighborhood before 1908 generally is of a folk, or simple vernacular, style. These houses, originally of rectangular shape, had no ornamentation. Various homeowners made additions over the years, so many homes have taken on other shapes. While a few of the homes are of a single story, most have one-and-a-half or two. Residents sometimes refer to a house of this type as the "original farmhouse." Few, if any, were farmhouses, though they are of the simple style common in early 20th century rural homes. About 7 percent (500) of Longfellow's homes were built during that period, but even at the height of dairy farming no more than 15 or 20 dwellings housed farmers of any kind.

A good example is the home at 3216 43rd Avenue, right, first owned by James Stanley, a florist. The earliest part of the house was small and had no basement. The house now shows four additions or modifications made between 1912 and 1928. The pay-as-you-go approach was common for houses built during the period.

After 1908, various cottage- and bungalow-style construction predominated. From about 1908 to 1915, one-and-a-half-story cottage designs like the one in *Walton's Home Builder* ad were common. But many variations on that theme, plus others styles, were built too. After 1915, the bungalow dominated, and by 1920, most of the new homes built in the neighborhood were bungalows.

A rectangular shape, one or one-and-a-half stories, and wide, open eaves define the bungalow, at least the ones in Longfellow. Its shape is well suited to the narrow, urban lots of the neighborhood; most orient with the narrow end to the street. Many early 20th-century plan books featured inexpensive bungalow designs easily built by a local carpenter or even the potential homeowner.

◀ 3216 43rd Avenue, 2008. No farmers ever lived in this "farm" style house built in 1907.

Developers like Walton had their own design books from which customers could choose a plan for a home. Some people ordered kit homes from companies like Sears, Roebuck, and Company, which delivered the kit to the building site, ready to assemble. Sears offered kit homes in a wide variety of styles between 1908 and 1940.

3104 42nd Avenue, 1918. The Confer Brothers sales sign reads: "This thoroly [sic] modern six room bungalow for quick sale – price terms and inspection 'Confer with Confer.' " ▶

On nearly every block, one or two houses stick out from their neighbors. One such home is the "garage house" at 3520 44th Avenue, below. For many of these the story goes the original owner could not afford a full-sized house and so built a garage in which to live at the back of the lot. A full-sized house at the front of the lot never came to be.

While categorization of the homes in Longfellow is daunting, the variety in age and style ensures that every block is unique.

A "garage house" at 3520 44th Avenue, 2008 (built 1924) ▶

Public Schools

The construction of public school buildings closely followed periods of rapid residential development. The two main periods of school building mirror the pre-1920 and 1920s building booms. Simmons, Johnson, Hiawatha, and the new Longfellow School were built before 1920 while Cooper, Howe, Sanford, Dowling, and Stowe Schools appeared in the 1920s boom. Only Longfellow, Hiawatha, Dowling, and Sanford function as schools today.

Pre-1920 Schools

Longfellow (1918) at 31st Street and 31st Avenue is the second Longfellow School in the neighborhood, the first having opened earlier at Lake and Minnehaha (see chapter 3, pages 34–35).

◀ Longfellow School Decoration Day parade, c. 1923

Simmons opened as an elementary school at 38th Street and Minnehaha Avenue in 1905. Edward Somerby Stebbins, architect for the Minneapolis Board of Education from 1897 to 1912, designed the school, named for Henry Simmons, a popular Unitarian minister who died in 1905. Simmons was in session until 1939; Northwest Electronics Institute operated there after World War II until 1982. In the mid-1980s, the building was converted to apartments, still in use today.

Johnson School, named for Gov. John A. Johnson, who died in office in 1909, opened in 1910 between 37th and 38th Avenues, 31st and 32nd Streets. It was active until 1942. After World War II, various private vocational training

◀ Johnson School, 3100 38th Avenue, 1929

Building Longfellow ■ 87

Tug-of-war at Sanford School, c. 1935

schools rented the building. The last of these closed in 1976, and the building was torn down to make way for housing on the block.

Hiawatha School, named for the hero in Longfellow's poem *The Song of Hiawatha*, was built in 1916 at 42nd Avenue and 42nd Street. Hiawatha and the new Longfellow are good examples of the "California Plan" of school design, emphasizing light, air, and outdoor access to each classroom. The one-story design features classrooms with windows and doors to an interior courtyard or space for indoor recreation such as a gym.

1920s Schools

Cooper Elementary School, named for 19th-century author James Fenimore Cooper, was built at 33rd Street and 44th Avenue in 1923. Howe Elementary School, named for Julia Ward Howe, author of "The Battle Hymn of the Republic," was built at 38th Street and 43rd Avenue in 1928. Sanford Junior High, named for Maria Louise Sanford, the first woman professor at the University of Minnesota, was built at 36th Street and 42nd Avenue in 1926. All these schools are two- or three-story brick structures using standardized Minneapolis Board of Education plans. Both Cooper and Howe closed in 2005, and the future use of the buildings remains uncertain.

Stowe School, named for abolitionist Harriet Beecher Stowe, opened as a "temporary" wood-sided school at the southeast corner of 28th Street and 40th Avenue. Built in 1923, it remained in session until 1942. An apartment building until 1959, it then was torn down to make way for single-family homes.

Industry

Minneapolis, known historically as the grain-milling capital of the world, is less well known for its role in the agricultural implement industry. From the 1870s, Minneapolis was the home of farm-implement companies making tractors, threshing machines, and the like. As more and more land came under cultivation to supply the city's flourmills, the demand for agricultural implements increased. What is now the collective site of Target, Cub Foods, Minnehaha Mall, and their acres of parking saw successive generations of implement- and steel-manufacturing companies between 1873 and 1972.

Longfellow played a part in the grain trade as well. The industry started to move from the Falls of St. Anthony in the 1880s, and grain elevators soon arose in the neighborhood. Inexpensive land and good rail service along modern-day Hiawatha Avenue allowed for the development of a line of grain elevator "skyscrapers" along the western edge of Longfellow. Beginning about 1915, flour and feed mills operated in the same area for many of the same reasons.

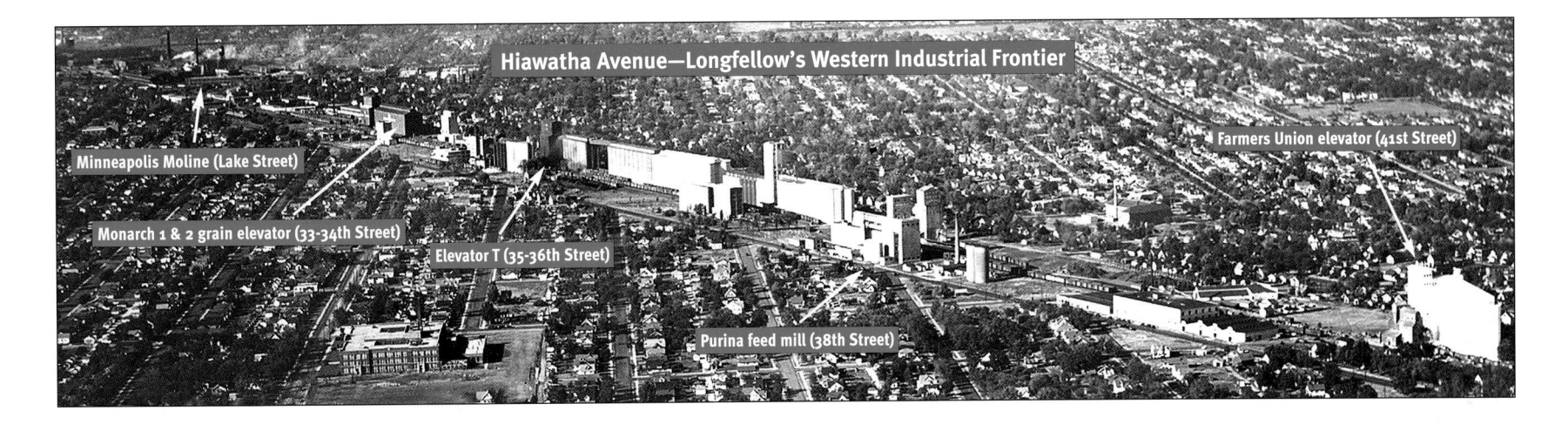

Looking north at the east side of Hiawatha Avenue, c. 1931

Minneapolis Harvester Works

Minneapolis Harvester Works opened in 1873 on the west side of Minnehaha Avenue from about 28th to 29th Streets, along the Milwaukee, St. Paul and Minneapolis railroad tracks. Dorilus Morrison (1814–1897), Minneapolis's first mayor, was one of the businessmen establishing the firm, which made reaping machinery. When the factory burned to the ground in 1876, the owners immediately rebuilt. In 1880 the plant employed 200 men and produced 2,600 units total of three models of harvesting machinery.

The factory was far from the built-up area of Minneapolis, so most of the workers and their families lived in Longfellow's first subdivision, South Minneapolis, platted by Morrison in 1873. The factory prospered during the first half of the 1880s, but it closed down in the late 1880s, and Walter A. Wood Harvester Company of St. Paul bought it out in 1892.

The site sat vacant through the 1890s, with the buildings used for storage. In 1900 a spectacular fire destroyed several of the larger buildings. The dilapidated buildings and fire-scorched site, however, did not sit vacant for long.

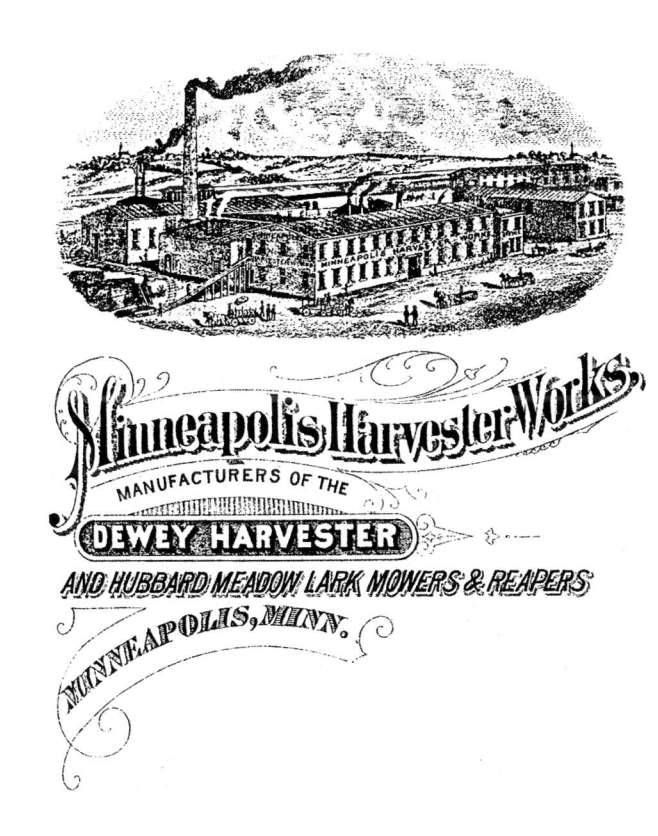

◀ Images from a Minneapolis Harvester Works letterhead, c. 1879. The street at bottom right of the drawing is Minnehaha Avenue.

Building Longfellow ■ 89

Team of 10 horses moving a large beam at Minneapolis Steel and Machinery, c. 1905. This explains the origin of the term "horsepower." ▶

Interior, Minneapolis Steel and Machinery, 1907 ▶

Minneapolis Steel and Machinery

By the time the Minneapolis Steel and Machinery Company (MSMC) formed in 1902, the Harvester Works site had been empty for a number of years. MSMC was able to buy the land from the Hennepin County Auditor for back taxes—at a small fraction of its worth. Besides getting the land nearly for free, the buyer gained a number of buildings left from Harvester Works for use in its new enterprise.

MSMC brought together the interests of two companies—Twin City Iron Works and Minnesota Malleable Iron Company—with those of James L. Record (previously involved in the development of grain elevators). MSMC intended to create a wide range of metal products including engines, boilers, mining machinery and equipment, all classes and kinds of implements and machinery, millwright and mill-furnishing work, and architectural and structural steel. MSMC grew quickly. By 1908 it had its own line of tractors, and by 1913 it was making tractors for other companies.

90 ■ The Neighborhood by the Falls

◀ Women making parts for the Twin City tractor line at Minneapolis Steel and Machinery, c. 1917

About this time MSMC incorporated a subsidiary, Toro, to make engines for Bull Tractor Company. During World War I, production and employment increased dramatically to fill contracts for shells and other war materiel for the United States and other countries. For the first time, women worked on the shop floor, to ramp up production and fill vacancies left by men gone off to war.

In spring and summer 1916 a bitter strike—the start of labor troubles at MSMC and later at Minneapolis-Moline—occurred. At the start of the strike, organized labor labeled MSMC's top management, including George M. Gillette and J. L. Record, as a villain and an "eternal opponent of labor." The labor press of the time is full of strong rhetoric against MSMC management for its poor

Building Longfellow ■ 91

A lockout by management started a strike at Minneapolis Steel and Machinery Company, 1916.

Minneapolis Steel and Machinery 12-20 tractors and threshers on flatcars ready for shipping, c. 1919. The building at center is the Monarch grain elevator, the first one in the neighborhood. ▶

treatment of workers and low wages. Regardless of the jobs brought by war, organized labor was against the war and saw MSMC as part of the problem.

Near the end of the war, 6,000 employees of MSMC established their own cooperative buying club—Longfellow Mercantile Company—at the plant; the MSMC management set up a cafeteria. Former president Theodore Roosevelt visited the plant in October 1918 to encourage workers to buy U.S. war bonds. After the war ended, MSMC entered the small tractor market, but the agricultural recession of the early 1920s took its toll. MSMC employment plummeted, inching up in the late 1920s to 1,200.

Minneapolis-Moline

In 1926 W. C. MacFarlane took over as general manager and president of MSMC, then oversaw the merger joining MSMC, Minneapolis Threshing Machine Company, and Moline Implement Company to create Minneapolis-Moline. Given the tough economic climate, the merger was essential to saving the business of all three. After the merger, the Lake Street plant specialized in the production of tractors and engines. Minneapolis-Moline prospered in the 1930s and 1940s, producing many wartime products, including the original Jeep.

The plant expanded during the 1920s, eventually filling the entire area from Lake Street to about 28th Street, Minnehaha west to Hiawatha Avenue. Strikes took place at the plant during the 1930s, and labor troubles continued

◀ Minneapolis-Moline Tractor Model Jeep with military wheels, carrying the Minneapolis-Moline Fire Brigade alongside the factory, c. 1943

after World War II. In a contentious two-month strike in 1946, workers ground Lake Street traffic to a halt several times in protest. Nevertheless, sales soared in the late 1940s, and innovations in the 1950s kept the company strong. Nearly 6,300 employees total worked in the Minneapolis, Hopkins, Moline (Illinois), and Louisville (Kentucky) plants in 1954.

In 1962 White Motor Company of Lansing, Michigan, acquired Minneapolis-Moline. Changing profitability and a greater emphasis by White Motor on truck production meant closing the Minneapolis plant in 1972. Unable to find a buyer for the old factory buildings, the owners in June 1973 demolished and hauled away the debris of all 15 buildings on the site.

◀ Minneapolis-Moline JTS tractor, 1935

Building Longfellow ■ 93

Aerial view, Minneapolis-Moline factory complex, 1938. No camera could capture the massive site from any other perspective. Today's Cub Foods would be at upper right, Target at the site of the large building at lower left. ▶

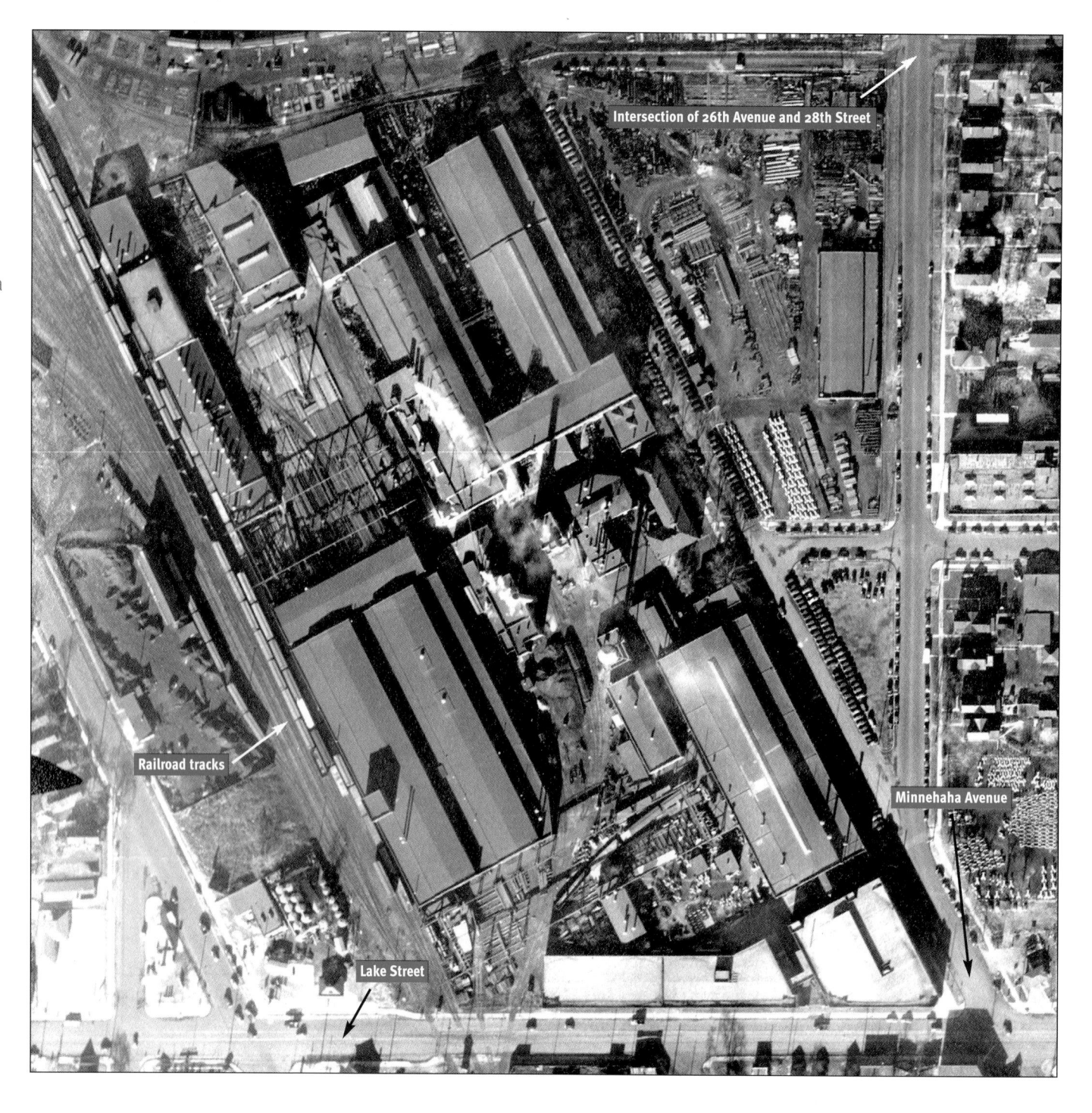

94 ■ The Neighborhood by the Falls

Grain Elevators

Longfellow's grain elevators—its tallest buildings by far—stand watch at the western edge of the neighborhood along Hiawatha Avenue. Minneapolis has a long history as a center of milling and grain trade, but the industry began to move from the area of the Falls of St. Anthony in the late 1800s, and grain elevators then rose in Longfellow.

The elevators depended and still depend on railroads to haul grain in and out. The Chicago, Milwaukee, and St. Paul Railway (CM&StP, commonly known as the Milwaukee Road) served these elevators. The track for this line, laid in 1864, was well developed when the first elevators appeared. With rail service and inexpensive land along the tracks, Longfellow was a logical place for these giants.

Grain companies established elevators in Longfellow primarily to store grain awaiting transport to mills, but many elevators also improved grain quality through cleaning, sorting, and drying. All of the grain elevators in the neighborhood are on the east side of the CM&StP tracks, fronting on Dight Avenue, and running nearly a mile from 33rd to 41st Streets.

D. A. Martin built the first grain elevator in Longfellow in 1888, just south of 33rd Street on the east side of the CM&StP tracks. Nearly 13 stories tall, it must have been visible for miles in that sparsely settled section of Minneapolis. By 1894 Monarch Elevator Company owned this elevator and built the much-larger Monarch No. 2 next to it. By 1900, there were five, mostly small, grain elevators stretching from 33rd to 41st Streets.

Most of the elevator sites of today were previously the sites of smaller ones—more like the country elevators now found in rural areas and small towns. Made of wood, they had steel or iron siding and were prone to fire. The tallest part was the "elevator"—containing equipment to get the grain to the top of the bins in the shorter parts of the building.

Later elevators consisted of one building with elevating equipment serving a series of shorter storage tanks by conveyor belts. Most of the Longfellow elevators stored grain for the milling or brewing industry, though a small Cargill elevator near 34th Street processed and stored seed grain. Newer elevators replaced the early ones, which were mostly torn down by 1930. The last standing were Monarch 1 and 2, operating into the 1960s but demolished in 1974.

In 1899, the world's first reinforced-concrete grain elevator went up in St. Louis Park. Little time passed before concrete was the preferred material for grain elevators. Longfellow's first concrete grain elevators went up in 1908; they are still in use near 35th Street and Dight Avenue. A grain-elevator building boom in the 1920s saw the replacement of many of the old wood elevators, and by 1930, all the grain elevators seen today were part of the

Monarch Elevator Company, 1905

Cargill's Elevator T complex, 35th and Dight, 1931, showing the progression from the 14-story, highest-in-the-neighborhood, wood elevator (1901) to shorter and more durable concrete grain bins (1908 and 1917). ▶

Longfellow scene. Grain-storage capacity grew a phenomenal 700 percent from 1900 to 1930, making Longfellow one of the major grain-handling-and-storage areas of the city.

Most of the elevators built along Hiawatha Avenue ended up in the hands of large grain and milling conglomerates, such as Archer-Daniels-Midland (ADM) and Cargill, with one exception—the Farmers Union Elevator at 41st and Dight. This substantial Farmers Union Terminal Association (FUTA, 1930) holding was an outgrowth of the farmer-owned elevator movement that had overtaken the country-elevator scene in the 1920s. When a new, consolidated organization (Farmers Union Grain Terminal Association, known as FUGTA or simply GTA) formed in 1938, it was a force to reckon with. GTA quickly encountered

96 ■ The Neighborhood by the Falls

Farmers Union Elevator, 41st and Dight, 1931. This elevator, simply added to the old Minnehaha elevator, used its train shed and elevator.

stiff opposition from the large grain companies that thought cooperative grain marketing was socialist and un-American. The cooperative hung on largely through the efforts of its founder, Bill Thatcher, and his government connections including those with Presidents Franklin Delano Roosevelt and John F. Kennedy. GTA later became Harvest States Cooperatives; in 2008 its elevator sits empty, awaiting redevelopment of the site.

The Quigley family worked at the Farmers Union Elevator, helping to build it in the late 1920s and working there after World War II, for nearly 50 years. Allen Quigley, the last one in the family to work at the elevator, remembers going with his father, James (who helped build it), as a child to catch pigeons at the elevator to bring home and cook for dinner. Allen and his four brothers worked at the mill— Allen starting as a machine operator in the mid-1950s and working his way to manager before he retired in the early 1990s. He recalls that the business, automated with computers starting in the 1970s, let 200 people go in the early 1980s as a result of that and problems in the grain trade. Automated elevators made the jobs of those such as grain shovelers and dust collectors obsolete.

All the other grain elevators visible today are active. Owned by General Mills, they stretch from 35th to 38th Streets along Dight Avenue. Longfellow's grain elevators are the dramatic and living legacy of Minneapolis's grain trading and milling industry. One thing for sure, with all the grain stored in the area, no one in Longfellow should go hungry. If all of the grain currently stored in neighborhood elevators were milled into flour, it would be enough to make 241 million loaves of bread!

Minneapolis Milling Company played up its south-side location and hometown pride, c. 1930. ▶

Minnehaha Elevator, 41st and Dight, 1911, of the small "country" type ▶

Mills

As the waterpower at the Falls of St. Anthony became less important to millers, the milling industry was free to move anywhere with rail access. Steam-powered mills sprang up outside the St. Anthony milling district about the time of World War I; soon the good rail access along Hiawatha Avenue attracted mills to the neighborhood.

All the Longfellow mills were on the west side of the CM&StP tracks because the grain elevators filled much of the land on the east, and the mills needed access to a major road such as Hiawatha Avenue. Longfellow had three mills—two flourmills and a feed mill. Two were at 38th Street, the other at 35th.

Minneapolis Milling Company, which became Washburn Crosby Company, which became General Mills, put its mill into operation at the southeast corner of 35th and Hiawatha in 1914. Always a flourmill, it has changed little in appearance since the late 1920s. In addition to its well-known Miss Minneapolis brand, the mill produced new and innovative products such as Sunfed Flour, a 1930s innovation with a vitamin-D supplement. The mill, now owned by ADM, is still active.

98 ■ The Neighborhood by the Falls

◀ Minneapolis Milling Company, c. 1927

At the northeast corner of 38th and Hiawatha, the Atkinson Mill had produced flour since 1915. The mill and shorter grain elevators were built in 1915, the larger bins near 37th Street in 1939. The mill in 1951 had a maximum capacity of 1,000 barrels or about 200,000 pounds per day. Owned by ADM, this mill also is active today.

Across 38th Street on the southeast corner of the intersection is the only closed mill in the neighborhood. Originally home to the Clarx Milling Company, it was built in 1918, unusual in its status as a whole-wheat flourmill, unlike the other locals, which produced only white flour. Clarx survived only a few years, closing in 1921.

In 1923, Ralston Purina bought the site and started producing flour and cereal products. By the mid-1930s, Purina had converted the plant to a feed mill in which it produced its famous Chow line of animal feed. In 1951,

◀ Bagging equipment at Atkinson Milling Company, 3745 Hiawatha Avenue, 1957. The workers' hats read "Play Safe—Be Safe."

Building Longfellow ■ 99

Purina Mills, 1951 ▶

the plant reached its maximum capacity of 250 tons of feed per day. The plant closed in 2004. A developer who hopes to clear the site and build a retail-and-apartment complex similar in scale to the old mill buildings has purchased the site.

Research into the historic significance of the buildings indicates that the buildings replacing the oldest ones in the complex are too new to be eligible for designation by the National Register of Historic Places. Still, Longfellow is the only place left in Mill City with an appreciable concentration of active grain elevators and flourmills, a tangible reminder of the industry that made Minneapolis the center of industry and commerce it is today.

7/21st Century

21st Century

Rapid and dense redevelopment, rising property values, and major investments in public infrastructure have replaced the slow decline and suburban redevelopment of the last three decades of the 20th century. The rest of the world has discovered Longfellow.

Overleaf—
The Martin Olav Sabo Midtown Greenway bridge opened over Hiawatha Avenue in 2007.

West River Commons (2004), at Lake Street and West River Parkway, was the first large-scale neighborhood redevelopment project of the 21st century.
▼

Come along as we enjoy a summer day in 2007. You are part of a family cruising on a four-seat rental bike along the West River Parkway bike path. Hear the bells of an ice-cream truck as it moves slowly through the neighborhood. Lake Street during rush-hour traffic. Watch the light-rail trains come and go from the elevated Lake Street station. Or share the Midtown Greenway with a freight train as you bike along. See kids playing in the wading pool at Brackett, Hiawatha, or Longfellow Parks, and go ahead, put your feet in. Sit on the observation deck and watch a barge maneuver through Lock and Dam No. 1. This is the Longfellow neighborhood at the dawn of the 21st century —where much has changed, yet so much remains the same.

The theme thus far in 21st-century Longfellow is revitalization. Rapid and dense redevelopment, rising property values, and major investments in public infrastructure have replaced the slow decline and suburban redevelopment of the last three decades of the 20th century. The rest of the world has discovered Longfellow, which has driven up property values, encouraged redevelopment of old industrial sites, and caused a general reinvestment in the housing stock of the neighborhood. As businesses leave the neighborhood, new ones quickly replace them, unlike previous decades during which storefronts sat vacant for long periods or were converted to housing. New Hispanic and East African immigrants have contributed to this revitalization by opening stores along commercial corridors like Minnehaha Avenue and Lake Street.

Major Infrastructure Investments

East Lake Street Reconstruction

Lake Street was one of the first paved streets in the neighborhood. Streetcar tracks laid to 31st Avenue for the Wonderland Park opening in 1905 were extended to the Lake Street Bridge in 1906. The tracks lay in the middle of the street, a set for each direction embedded in large granite cobblestones. The city paved the rest of the street with bricks to the curb in 1909.

The last of the streetcars disappeared from Lake Street in 1954. Minneapolis did little conversion of the street to a four-lane roadway other than to pave over the cobblestones and streetcar tracks with asphalt. The road deteriorated despite several repavements and became increasingly difficult to keep in decent repair. By the late 1990s, government officials concluded that the entire roadway from Dupont Avenue to the Mississippi River must be rebuilt from the bottom up. That meant digging 15 feet in places, replacing waterlines, and constructing a totally new roadbed, paving, sidewalks, curbs, and gutters.

After years of planning, Lake Street reconstruction in the Longfellow neighborhood began in the spring of 2006 at Hiawatha Avenue. Officials considered a variety of roadway configurations. Early plans for a three-lane Lake Street, with east- and westbound lanes divided by a middle turn lane, gained significant support. Businesses raised the most objection, arguing that three lanes would restrict traffic and make it more difficult for shoppers to get to their businesses.

Ultimately a replication of the existing four-lane configuration trumped the three-lane concept. Construction proceeded with one side of the street rebuilt as the other supported two lanes of traffic. Metro Transit buses rerouted to 31st Street during construction season, as Lake Street was too narrow then to accommodate them.

The right-of-way for Lake Street in Longfellow is 20 feet wider than for Lake west of Hiawatha. This allowed for much more landscaping along the corridor and a variety of pavement and landscaping treatments tailored to adjacent businesses. Businesses and property owners along the street paid for enhanced streetscape elements such as benches and parking-lot screening with additional assessments. Many parking lots and used-car lots along the street moved into compliance with current zoning regulations with the addition of decorative fencing and landscaping on their Lake Street boundaries. Some of these landscaped/fenced areas included rain gardens to clean and slow runoff from adjacent paved areas. The enhanced streetscape elements helped to beautify and give the previously rundown thoroughfare a more uniform look.

Looking west from Lake Street Bridge in 2007, when Lake Street was still under construction

Workers tearing up the road for reconstruction unearthed a treasure trove of historic objects. In the evenings, after construction crews were gone, people from across the city swarmed the site, coming with cars, pickup trucks, trailers, and even wagons to pillage the rubble piles. They collected and hauled away valuable cobblestones and red bricks, much of which now graces the small pathways, patios, and garden surroundings of homes throughout the city. The old streetcar tracks, seen on side streets at the start of deconstruction, were too heavy to cart away.

While excitement about the reconstruction of Lake Street was evident among most residents, the businesses took a hit financially in two ways. They had to pay much of the assessment to beautify the area, and they endured a decrease in customer traffic as consumers avoided the construction area. One business claimed a 50 percent drop in revenue during construction. Most businesses, with the exception of the bars also hit hard by the smoking ban, seem to have done okay. The Lake Street Council (a Lake Street business group) offered assistance to affected businesses, and most Lake Street business owners figured out ways to weather the storm. Major reconstruction of the street in the Longfellow neighborhood ended in 2007, with finishing touches applied in early summer 2008.

The Midtown Greenway

The Midtown Greenway is a bicycle and pedestrian path crossing south Minneapolis, just north of Lake Street from the city's western border to the Mississippi River. Lit at night, plowed in the winter, and open year round, it runs in an old railroad corridor purchased by the Hennepin County Regional Rail Authority for eventual transit use. The Longfellow section, however, is unlikely to be used for transit.

The first part of the greenway, the segment from Fifth Avenue west to the city limits, opened in 2000. The segment from Fifth to Hiawatha Avenues opened in 2005, and the Longfellow/Seward section, from Hiawatha Avenue to West River Parkway, opened in 2006. The Midtown Greenway forms the boundary between the Longfellow and Seward neighborhoods (roughly parallel to 27th Street) and crosses an industrial area featuring Brackett Park and Anne Sullivan School as major landmarks on the Longfellow side.

The Canadian Pacific Railroad owns the tracks in the Longfellow/Seward section; the Minnesota Commercial

Looking east down the rail corridor in the vicinity of 28th Avenue, 2001 ▶

Looking east, down the completed greenway trails in the vicinity of 28th Avenue, 2008 ▶

Railroad runs freight trains twice a day on the tracks—one train in and one train out. A fence separates the trails from the tracks; Hennepin County owns only the trails portion of the corridor.

Federal alternative transportation funds, plus Hennepin County and City of Minneapolis funds to a smaller degree, underwrote construction of the greenway. The Longfellow Community Council allocated $150,000 of its Neighborhood Revitalization Program Phase I dollars towards greenway improvements. These funds made possible the addition to the original plans of a ramp at Brackett Park, plus the creation of a native-plant landscaping plan and several landscaping projects based on it.

Before construction of the greenway, dense, weedy vegetation covered much of the corridor. Implementation of the landscape plan meant an improvement in appearance as well as a decrease in crime in the area. The City of Minneapolis approved $75,000 for the installation of public art in 2008 at five locations in the Longfellow/Seward section of the greenway. A spectacular cable-stay bridge over Hiawatha Avenue, the first one of its type in Minnesota, opened on November 10, 2007, to provide greenway users a safe and quick way over Hiawatha Avenue. The bridge is named for Congressman Martin Sabo, who secured federal funds for the $2.9 million bridge. The bridge, an artistic work in itself, is hard to miss, especially at night, when a blue-tinted light illuminates its 100-foot-high mast.

Since it is an old rail corridor, the Midtown Greenway has few street crossings, making it a fast and hassle-free way to bicycle across the city, a major route for biking commuters and recreational cyclists alike. At the west end of the greenway, it hooks up with the Southwest LRT trail, which leads far into the western suburbs—to Lake Minnetonka and beyond. The greenway connects to Chain of Lakes and Grand Rounds on the west end and again at the eastern terminus of West River Parkway.

Provided that the plans satisfy a myriad interests and jurisdictions, the route will cross the Mississippi River over a new bridge somewhere in the vicinity of the current Short Line railroad bridge.

Planning is underway on the St. Paul (east) side of the river to connect the greenway to points east in that city. The Midtown Greenway, a transportation alternative to the newly reconstructed Lake Street, provides a pleasant and safe place to bike and walk along the northern end of the neighborhood.

Highway 55 and Light Rail

The 21st century saw the final chapter of a long saga involving the rebuilding of Hiawatha Avenue and the implementation of light rail transit (LRT). Hiawatha Avenue (also known as Highway 55) forms the western border of the greater Longfellow community and connects the southeastern suburbs to downtown. From 1998 to 2004, there was always some section of the corridor under construction, first for a new four-lane roadway and then for LRT.

Work on the project began with the bridge over Highway 62 at the far southern end of the project. The "reroute" plan called for redirection of the roadway east towards the Mississippi River and closer to the resources of historic Fort Snelling, taking some land from Minnehaha Park. The lost parkland was reclaimed in a "land bridge" over Hiawatha on the western edge of the park, near Minnehaha Creek and the site of the early 20th-century Longfellow Gardens. The new roadbed in the Longfellow section of the roadway followed the existing road so had little impact on property, business, or industry in the corridor.

While reconstruction was to improve the flow of traffic and access to the area, some citizens opposed the reroute because it required the removal of a grove of four oak trees said by some to be of special meaning to Dakota

Hiawatha Light Rail train, running by a prime redevelopment site, the old Purina feed mill at 38th Street, c. 2006

people. Although the protesters pursued many avenues in their attempt to stop the project, the effort failed and the reroute continued.

Shortly after the Hiawatha reroute work was complete, work on the light rail line began, on January 17, 2001. The line opened on June 26, 2004, initially running from downtown Minneapolis to Fort Snelling. Six months later the rest of the line opened, taking passengers all the way to the airport and the Mall of America. Twenty-four cars ran on the line. Construction costs totaled $715.3 million from federal, state, regional, and county sources. The new timing of stoplights along Hiawatha and at cross streets (such as 35th and 42nd Streets) gave preference to the light rail. Officials worked out some problems with long waits for drivers at the cross streets during the line's first year of operation.

Light-rail ridership immediately exceeded projections, with ridership 60 percent above expectations during the first year and 20 percent higher for the two years following. In 2007, the line carried 9.1 million passengers and averaged 27,000 riders per weekday, exceeding pre-construction ridership projections for as far ahead as 2020 by 8 percent. Critics, however, were quick to point out that even with high ridership numbers, the line needed a hefty yearly subsidy and that the money might be better spent on a new highway lane that would move more people. Supporters of LRT counter that this public service provides a valuable alternative form of transportation and reduces traffic congestion.

The neighborhoods on both sides of Hiawatha looked at LRT as an opportunity for more intense, transit-oriented development. Housing projects built along the line include several mixed-use condominium projects along the east side of Hiawatha. The proposal for a mixed-use redevelopment project at the southeast corner of 38th and Hiawatha, the old Purina Mills site, if it comes to fruition, will provide the largest increase in housing so far.

Business Life

The Rise and Fall of the Resource Center of the Americas

The old "downtown Longfellow," 27th Avenue and Lake Street, was at a crossroads entering the 21st century. It was ready to succeed but was at great risk of failure. Several large commercial buildings at the intersection were in decline or in the process of renovation. The two-story brick building at 3012 27th Avenue was sitting vacant—a one-story building attached to its south side housed a business called Sauna 27. At the time, street-front saunas had become synonymous with prostitution, and Longfellow residents had successfully pushed out other saunas along Lake Street. Sauna 27 was a notable holdout, highly visible at 27th Avenue and Minnehaha.

The neighborhood succeeded in shutting down Sauna 27 in 1999. A few years earlier, the Resource Center of the Americas, a group focused on Latin American political and social issues such as free trade, was looking for a larger space for its headquarters. After the group found the two-story building, the Longfellow Community Council (LCC) granted the Resource Center $100,000 to renovate the structure and move its operations there. The LCC grant included funding for demolition of the old Sauna 27 building and conversion of the space to a plaza.

In 2001 the directors of the Resource Center voted to create a mosaic covering the north wall of the building, which faces a parking lot. They brought in Mexican artists to review the site. After intense study the artists agreed to do the work but suggested using the south wall, facing what would become the plaza. They worked on the *Mosaic of the Americas* for several months using donated tiles and the assistance of more than 100 volunteers. Shortly after the mosaic was complete, the plaza was built. The revitalized building and plaza helped start a business revival in the area.

The two-story Resource Center of the Americas building boasted a bookstore, café, and library and offered a variety of Spanish-language and other related classes. Grant funds supplemented the income from these ventures, but the organization struggled to make ends meet. In 2004 it resorted to layoffs to balance the budget. The center's financial situation did not improve, and the board of directors voted to cease operations and put the building up for sale in August 2007. Nevertheless, the Resource Center of the Americas changed the face of 27th and Lake and was an integral part in reestablishing the commercial district as a vibrant place to shop and eat.

International Influence

Immigrants have impacted the Longfellow neighborhood, particularly on East Lake Street, where multiple Latino businesses, for example, have taken root on the corridor. In 2000, Radio Rey, an all-Spanish radio station located at Minnehaha Avenue and Lake Street, moved its frequency to 630 AM radio and began broadcasting 24 hours, seven days a week, to meet the needs of the growing Latino population.

◀ The Resource Center of the Americas plaza features *Mosaic of the Americas: Many Strengths, Many Struggles*, a tile mosaic utilizing the azulejo technique.

Shortly thereafter, Longfellow saw the opening of several Latino businesses on East Lake. El Norteno, a longtime Mexican restaurant and market at 40th and Lake was joined by two other Hispanic establishments at 27th and Lake—the El Rodeo nightclub in the Oddfellows Building and Manny's Tortas, a gourmet Mexican sandwich shop in the Coliseum Building. Rainbow Foods and Cub Foods recognized the influx of Latinos in the neighborhood. Cub modified its in-store signage to read in both Spanish and English, and both stores created significant sections featuring Mexican foods.

The growth of Latino businesses in the area leveled off rather quickly, as some businesses closed or left the area. After only a few years, CLUES, a Hispanic nonprofit social service organization that assisted Latino families from the Coliseum Building, moved out of the neighborhood. The same went for La Clinica en Lake, a medical clinic focusing on the Latino community. Los Gallos, a money-transfer company at 27th and Lake, closed its doors and moved closer to the core of the Hispanic community near Chicago Avenue and Lake Street.

Poodle Club, 3001 East Lake, 2005 ▶

El Norteno, 4000 East Lake Street— a Mexican restaurant and market, 2008

While Latinos have had a lasting impact, many other cultural groups also influence and enrich the area. Longfellow has been home to ethnic eateries including ⁰a Japanese sushi, Chinese, Thai, and Greek restaurants as well as an Ethiopian bar.

The End of the Workingman's Bar

Forces have conspired to close down some longtime working-class bar/restaurants in the neighborhood. Major reconstruction of Lake Street, starting in 2006, hit all its businesses, including restaurants, with higher assessments and decreased patronage.

Another factor affecting patronage was the smoking ban enacted in Hennepin County in 2005. Smokers were quick to cross the Mississippi River to patronize eating and drinking establishments in nearby St. Paul (the ban did not extend statewide until 2007). Molly Quinn's, a blue-collar Irish drinking hole, recently removed from its longtime home at 43rd and Lake to 33rd and Lake, was the first to go. The Lake Street Garage, a restaurant known for its juicy burgers, pizza, and shakes, unable to recover, was the next. Then the Poodle Club, a dive at 3001 Lake Street known as a smoker's bar and famous for its low-cost, hearty meals, also closed. Smokers had come for dinner, staying for the evening, socializing over drinks, playing pool, and listening to the band in the back corner. Finally in late 2007, Popeye's, a drinking hole at 3601 East Lake, went out of business. Several other establishments along Minnehaha Avenue and elsewhere closed about the time of the 2005 smoking ban.

Some places have reopened smoke-free, under new management, and with a more modern theme. The old Poodle Club, now McMahon's Irish Pub, markets itself as the "world's first Irish blues bar." The 21st century has seen the end of the smoke-filled, working-class bar. Only time can tell whether its more modern replacements will take hold or some other spots will become the smoke-free hangouts of the era.

Neighborhood Livability

Longfellow is known for its quiet streets and livability. Through the Longfellow Community Council and other nonprofit organizations, residents work hard to maintain that livability. They have volunteered for projects and causes such as Mississippi River gorge plantings and quieting a noisy industrial neighbor. This interest has extended beyond the river to involvement in gardening efforts in resident's own yards that protect water quality and native ecosystems.

Rain Gardens

Many residents of Longfellow choose to live in the neighborhood because of its proximity to the Mississippi River and the parkland of the river gorge. Largely due to the interest of residents in watershed issues, Longfellow has been a leader in Minneapolis for encouraging residents and other property owners to landscape with native plants and to install rain gardens. Through the efforts of the Longfellow River Gorge Committee, several neighborhood initiatives have helped residents and businesses make their property more watershed friendly. Beginning in 2002, the Longfellow Community Council (LCC) sponsored

Groups like the Friends of the Mississippi River sponsor canoe trips on the Mississippi River that feature the Longfellow stretch of the river.

Birding hikes in the river gorge are a popular springtime event in the neighborhood.

21st Century ■ 109

Grant recipient Julia Vanatta showed off her rain garden at 3408 39th Avenue during the 2008 Watershed Friendly Yard Tour. ▶

Barr Engineering designed this rain garden, one of several on the site, to manage runoff from 95 percent of the parking lot and part of the 7-SIGMA building roof, 2005. ▶

matching-grant programs and workshops to teach people how they could reduce storm-water runoff using native plants, rain gardens, and rain barrels.

Why rain gardens? Every rain in the Longfellow neighborhood ultimately pollutes the Mississippi. Rain falls on the many hard surfaces of the urban landscape—roofs, streets, sidewalks, parking lots—and runs into the storm drains. As it travels down the alleys and streets, the water collects salt, oil, leaves, fertilizer, and other pollutants. Within minutes the city's storm sewers whisk this witch's brew directly to the river. Rain gardens offer a simple and effective way to help reduce urban storm-water runoff.

A rain garden soaks up rainwater mainly coming off a roof but also from a lawn. The garden is a shallow depression landscaped with wildflowers and other native vegetation, replacing some of the lawn. The garden fills with a few inches of water, allowing it to seep into the ground instead of running into storm drains. Compared with a conventional lawn, a rain garden allows about 30 percent more water to soak into the ground, usually in less than a few hours.

Using the city's Neighborhood Revitalization Program funds and grants from the Mississippi Watershed Management Organization, the Longfellow Community Council and the Seward Neighborhood Group awarded matching grants ranging from $50 to $250 for the purchase of native plants to 287 residents in Longfellow and Seward from 2002 to 2006. During the program's four years, LCC awarded $25,740 in matching grants, spurring a total investment of nearly $60,000 in native landscaping in the neighborhood.

The program included a two-part workshop taught by neighborhood resident Carolyn Carr of Ecological Strategies, LLC. This program was one of the most popular ever offered by LCC, with demand far exceeding availability in its first few years. More than 530 residents attending the workshop learned how to design and plant gardens using native plants. A yellow lawn sign designated the "Watershed Friendly Yard" of each resident installing native plantings or a rain garden. Since 2004, LCC has sponsored a Watershed Friendly Yard tour each summer to showcase a few of these yards, fostering greater awareness and appreciation of the benefits of native plants.

Neighborhood businesses and schools have also installed rain gardens. Starting in March 2005, the City of Minneapolis has charged owners a storm-water management fee according to the amount of impervious surface on their property. A credit program recognizes property owners who have installed rain gardens, green roofs, or other storm-water management practices improving water quality and reducing storm-water runoff. The program offers a 40 percent storm-water credit to property owners with large buildings or parking lots installing storm-water management projects utilizing "Best Management Practices." By the end of 2008, a total of seven commercial rain-garden projects were in motion the neighborhood, including two at neighborhood schools, one at the East Lake Library, several for businesses, and one for a small apartment building.

Together these yards and businesses not only help improve water quality but also increase habitat for birds and pollinators and make Longfellow a more beautiful place to live.

The Saga of Metro Produce

In 2006 Longfellow was host to a battle between public and private entities, resulting in a court decision powerful enough to affect cities nationwide. It all started in 2002, when a company called Metro Produce moved into the old Tiro Industries plant and warehouse on 28th Street and 27th Avenue. The site consists of two square blocks with a warehouse taking up the better part the western half; the eastern half is vacant. The warehouse is directly across the street from a residential area; Metro idled trucks on cold winter nights and ran coolers in summer. About 128 semi trucks came and went from the site each week, many of them at night.

◀ East half of Metro Produce site in 2001 before it was developed as a parking lot for a moving company.

The loading docks face south, right down 28th Avenue, a solid block of homes. Residents down the avenue felt they were bombarded with noise pollution through the day and, most egregiously, through the night. They quickly organized against the constant and all-night truck noise. Community meetings involving the company, the city, and area residents, resulted in the planting of a number of trees to soften the noise. When that didn't help much, the city placed no-parking signs along 28th Street. The drivers then parked on Metro Produce property just a few feet off the street, with little abatement of the noise.

Finally in 2005, Minneapolis Ninth Ward Councilman Gary Schiff drafted an ordinance prohibiting truck idling from 10 P.M. to 6 A.M. The ordinance resulted in citations issued to drivers idling at the site. Metro Produce fought back, suing the City of Minneapolis on grounds that the noise ordinance was unconstitutional. A federal judge granted an injunction, stopping enforcement of the ordinance. Six months later, another federal judge ruled the no-idling ordinance unconstitutional on grounds that it was too vague.

Metro Produce claimed that enforcement of the ordinance had caused it to fall behind in shipments and ultimately to the loss of a mushroom account. The city, having already lost the case, settled the lawsuit with payment to Metro Produce of $2.3 million.

As all this was in play, area neighbors were pushing conversion of the eastern (vacant) half of the property to NoLo (for North Longfellow) Park. They had plans drawn for a potential park and held discussions about the possibility with the landowner. Since the immediate area lacks the parkland that other parts of the neighborhood enjoy, residents were keen for park development. But negotiations with the landowner went nowhere, and the neighbors soon recognized that the owner wanted an industrial user for the valuable property. It has since been paved over for the storage of the trucks and trailers for a moving company, which has built a berm and installed landscaping on two sides of the property to provide shielding; it hasn't idled trucks late at night. That development of the property nevertheless ended the longstanding hope of area residents for a park on the site.

West side of Hiawatha Flats, 44th Street and Dight Avenue, 2008 ▶

Building Boom

In the new millennium, redevelopment projects expanded Longfellow's housing stock. Developers bought up empty or underutilized industrial and commercial lots and built multilevel condominiums and apartments. These projects utilized a variety of designs including mixed-use developments with retail and housing, loft apartments, luxury condominiums, and upscale and affordable apartments.

In 2002, construction started on the first major Longfellow redevelopment of the 21st century—West River Commons. Construction was progressing nicely on the mixed-use development, along Lake Street from West River Parkway to 46th Avenue, when tragedy struck. On the night of June 24, 2003, a fire, probably caused by lightning and fanned by high winds, quickly became a raging inferno. Sixty-four firefighters struggled through the night to bring the blaze under control. Strong winds blew the

◀ Looking west along Dorman Avenue near West River Parkway at the aftermath of the West River Commons fire, July 9, 2003

sparks to the northeast and across the alley, and the fire destroyed a duplex, four garages, and several parked cars and damaged two more homes.

Despite the fire, the project moved forward to completion in 2004. The City of Minneapolis and the Longfellow Community Council commissioned the sculpture *P.S. Wish You Were Here* for the plaza at the West River Parkway end of the development. Restaurants and businesses in the development have seen a brisk business.

Following the completion of the Hiawatha LRT line in 2004, several upscale developments arose near Hiawatha Avenue on previously underutilized industrial parcels near LRT stations. Transit Oriented Development (TOD) projects in Longfellow have included:

- 42nd Street Lofts, a small loft-style condominium development built in 2005 and 2006 at 42nd Street and Dight Avenue
- The Oaks Hiawatha Station, a 61-unit upscale apartment complex with first-floor retail, built on the corner of 46th Street and Snelling Avenue in 2005. In 2008, Snaps, a fitness center, occupied a portion of the retail space.
- Hiawatha Flats, a 160-unit upscale apartment complex at 44th Street and Dight Avenue, opened in 2007

Two affordable apartment projects—Trinity Apartments and Hiawatha Commons—rose during the boom. Holy Trinity Church built Trinity Apartments, a 24-unit apartment building, in 2003, on Lake Street at 28th Avenue. It has eight market-rate units, with the remaining units set aside for low-income or handicapped people. Hiawatha Commons, completed in 2006, is at the north end of the Target/Cub Foods parking lot near the corner of 28th and Minnehaha Avenues. The same group owning the nearby Minnehaha Mall owns the commons' first-floor retail space. Above the retail area are 80 affordable housing units, half of which are studio apartments; the rest are one- and two-bedroom apartments.

Still on the horizon (as of late 2008) was the Longfellow Station redevelopment project at the old Purina Mills site, 38th Street and Hiawatha Avenue. Developer Dale Joel of Capital City Growth has owned the site since shortly after the mill closed in 2004; his latest plans call for an apartment and retail complex. The Longfellow Community Council (LCC) has a Community Benefits Agreement with the developer, guaranteeing certain benefits for the community in exchange for LCC support. This is the first redevelopment project along the Hiawatha Avenue strip of grain elevators and mills south of 34th Street.

Some think the area is ripe for redevelopment, especially should the grain elevators close and the railroad tracks, which split the land between Hiawatha and Dight Avenues, be abandoned. Hennepin County, in conjunction with its Minnehaha Avenue reconstruction project, is currently studying the historic resources and development potential of the area.

In 2007 the housing market entered a slump, with the condominium market especially hard hit. At least one multiphase project completed its first phase only to cancel the next one due to the market slowdown. An upscale condominium project overlooking Minnehaha Park at 46th Street and 46th Avenue stalled in 2006 after construction of the foundation walls. Only time can tell whether these projects continue to completion or their sites lie empty until the next housing boom.

The Future

While the future is uncertain, Longfellow has so far been spared the worst of the home foreclosure crisis; home prices have been relatively stable. Whatever the future holds, Longfellow—with quiet streets, modest and sturdy housing, and central location—will weather this downturn much as it did the economic depression of the 1930s and remain an appealing place to live.

Dowling Community Garden, 2006 ▶

History presentation on Meeker Island Lock and Dam remnants, c. 2005. Groups like the Friends of the Mississippi River sponsor canoe trips on the Mississippi River, featuring history and natural-history interpretation. ▶

REFERENCES

Entries appear in the order of the subject matter of the text.

Abbreviations

Corps	U.S. Army Corps of Engineers
HQO	Heritage Quest Online census database
LM	*Longfellow Messenger*
LNM	*Longfellow Nokomis Messenger*
MCL	Minneapolis Central Library
MHS	Minnesota Historical Society
MH	*Minnesota History*
MJ	*Minneapolis Journal*
MSJ	*Minneapolis Star Journal*

Introduction

Glenna, Tom. "Hiawatha Notebook." *LNM*, August 2007, p. 4.

The East Lake Shopper, a mid-1930s newspaper covering Lake Street roughly from Bloomington Avenue to the Mississippi River often referred to that area as "Southtown."

Chapter 1: Mighty Mississippi . . .

Mississippi River Commission, Corps. *A Survey of the Mississippi River, Chart No. 189.* N.p.: The author, 1899.

Native Vegetation

"Boy and Wheelbarrow Have to Bring Home the Family Bacon; Delivery Wagons Balked by Mud in this Minneapolis Highway." *Minneapolis Tribune*, September 9, 1913, p. 15.

Petersen, William J. *Mississippi River Panorama: Henry Lewis Great National Work.* Iowa City, IA: Clio, 1979.

Stevens, John. *Personal Recollections of Minnesota and its People, and Early History of Minneapolis.* Minneapolis: Tribune Job Printing, 1890.

Morris, Lucy Leavenworth Wilder, ed. *Old Rail Fence Corners: Frontier Tales Told by Minnesota Pioneers.* St. Paul: MHS Press, 1914 (1976 reprint). *See* recollections of Mrs. C. A. Smith (p. 141), James M. Gillespie (p. 75), Charles Bohanon (pp. 67–68), and Isaac Layman (p. 76).

"Those Were Wonderful Days: 40 Years Ago." *East Lake Shopper*, April 18 (p. 6) and 25 (p. 6), 1935. Available on microfilm at MHS, St. Paul.

Anfinson, John. O. *River of History: A Historic Resources Study of Mississippi National River and Recreation Area.* St. Paul: Corps, St. Paul District, 2003. *See* http://www.nps.gov/miss/historyculture/ ("Historic Resources Study").

Bratt, Carola. "Longfellow Neighbors, Victor Nelson: Minnehaha Dairy." *LNM*, January 1988, p. 3.

Smith, David C. *City of Parks: The Story of Minneapolis Parks.* Minneapolis: Minneapolis Park and Recreation Board, 2008.

Gorge Geology

For a sense of the size of the falls of the Glacial River Warren, *see* http://www.niagarafallslive.com/Facts_about_Niagara_Falls.htm (December 7, 2008).

Anfinson, John O. *River of History: A Historic Resources Study of Mississippi National River and Recreation Area.* St. Paul: Corps, St. Paul District, 2003. *See also* http://www.nps.gov/miss/historyculture/ ("Historic Resources Study").

Wild and Rugged River

Mississippi River Commission, Corps. *A Survey of the Mississippi River, Chart No. 189.* N.p.: The author, 1899.

"The 'Falls City.'" *St. Anthony Express*, July 14, 1855.

Winchell Trail

Upham, Warren. *Minnesota Geographic Names: Their Origin and Historic Significance.* St. Paul: MHS, 1920.

University of Minnesota Department of Geology and Geophysics. "Winchell Trail." *See* http://www.geo.umn.edu/Winchell_Trail.html (December 7, 2008).

Schwartz, George M. "Newton Horace Winchell: A Tribute." *See* http://www.geo.umn.edu/Winchell.html (December 6, 2008).

University of Minnesota Institute of Technology. "Commemorating 125 Years of Geology, 1874–1999." *See* hhtp://itdean.umn.edu/news/inventing/1999_Fall/geology.html (December 6, 2008).

Damming and Navigating the River

"An Act to Incorporate the Mississippi River Improvement and Manufacturing Company." *Minnesota Territorial Laws, 1857.* (Chapter LVIII [58], pp. 230–35.)

Anfinson, John O. *The River We Wrought.* Minneapolis: University of Minnesota Press, 2003.

——. "The Secret History of the Mississippi's Earliest Locks and Dams." *MH* (Summer 1995): 254–67.

——. "Hints of the Natural River." *St. Paul Pioneer Press*, September 26, 2007.

Lock and Dam No. 1

Anfinson, John O. *The River We Wrought.* Minneapolis: University of Minnesota Press, 2003.

——. "The Secret History of the Mississippi's Earliest Locks and Dams." *MH* (Summer 1995): 254–67.

What's in a Name? Meeker Island

Anfinson, John O. "The Secret History of the Mississippi's Earliest Locks and Dams." *MH* (Summer 1995): 254–67.

Warren, G. K. *Survey of the Upper Mississippi River.* Washington, DC: U.S. War Department, 1867. (Published in 39th Congress, 2nd Session, U.S. House of Representatives Ex. Doc. No. 58).

Works Progress Administration. *Minneapolis Aerial Photos.* 1938, No. 6-554. Available at the Borchert Map Library, Wilson Library, University of Minnesota.

Minnesota Department of Transportation. *Minnesota Aerial Photos.* 1955. Available at the Borchert Map Library, Wilson Library, University of Minnesota.

Short Line Railroad Bridge

Carole Zellie. *Midtown Greenway Historic Interpretation Panel at West River Parkway Ramp.* Text prepared for Hennepin County, MN, 2006.

Lake Street–Marshall Avenue Bridge

Historic American Engineering Record. *Lake Street–Marshall Avenue Bridge, HAER No. M–6.* Denver: National Park Service, December 1987.

Ford Bridge

Minneapolis City Directories, 1925–1980.

Interurbans Special No. 14—Electric Railways of Minneapolis & St. Paul. Los Angeles: Interurbans, 1953.

New Lake Street Bridge

Series of articles on the new Lake Street Bridge in *LM*: July 1987 (p. 1), September 1987 (p. 1), October 1987 (p. 1); and in its successor, *LNM*: May 1989 (p. 1), June 1990 (p. 1), and November 1992.

Pollution Problems

Metropolitan Drainage Commission of Minneapolis and St. Paul. *Second Report of the Metropolitan Drainage Commission of Minneapolis and St. Paul on the Subject of Sewage Disposal of Minneapolis, St. Paul, and Adjacent Areas, 1928.* St. Paul: The commission, 1929.

——. *Third Report of the Metropolitan Drainage Commission of Minneapolis and St. Paul on the Subject of Sewage Disposal of Minneapolis, St. Paul, and Adjacent Area for the Years 1929 and 1930.* St. Paul: The commission, 1931.

——. *Fourth Report of the Metropolitan Drainage Commission of Minneapolis and St. Paul on the Subject of Sewage Disposal of Minneapolis, St. Paul, and Adjacent Area for the Years 1931 and 1932.* St. Paul: The commission, 1933.

Recent River Gorge Restoration
Shaw, Daniel B. and Carolyn E. Carr. *Mississippi River Gorge (Lower Gorge) Ecological Inventory and Restoration Management Plan*. St. Paul: Great River Greening, 2002. See http://www.greatrivergreening.org/_downloads/Gorge_Management_Plan.pdf (December 7, 2008).
Mississippi National River and Recreation Area, National Park Service. "Mississippi River Gorge Habitat Restoration and Trail Rehabilitation: Longfellow." See http://www.nps.gov/miss/naturescience/prairestlong.htm (December 7, 2008).

Chapter 2: Early Settlement

Native Americans in the Area
Anfinson, John O. *River of History: A Historic Resources Study of Mississippi National River and Recreation Area*. St. Paul: Corps, St. Paul District, 2003. See http://www.nps.gov/miss/historyculture/ ("Historic Resources Study").
National Park Service, Mississippi National River and Recreation Area. "The Mississippi and Minnesota River Confluence." See http://www.nps.gov/miss/historyculture/confluence.htm (December 22, 2008).
Shakopee Mdewakanton Sioux Community. "Stewards of the Earth." See http://www.ccsmdc.org/stewards.html (December 27, 2008).
Ruvolo, David. "A Summary of Native American Religions." See http://are.as.wvu.edu/ruvolo.htm (December 22, 2008).
Pond, Samuel W. *Dakotas or Sioux in Minnesota as They Were in 1834*. St. Paul: MHS Press, 1908 (1986 reprint).
———. "Gathering from the Traditional History of the Mdewakanton Dakotas." *Dakota Friend* (May 1851).
Stevens, John. *Personal Recollections of Minnesota and its People, and Early History of Minneapolis*. Minneapolis: Tribune Job Printing, 1890.
Hall, Steve. *Fort Snelling: Colossus of the Wilderness*. St. Paul: MHS Press, 1987.

The Road to Fort Snelling
"Works Hard for Wider Streets." *MJ*, March 15, 1910, p. 9.
Kane, Lucile M. *The Falls of St. Anthony: The Waterfall that Built Minneapolis*. St. Paul: MHS Press, 1987.

White Settlement Begins
Kane, Lucile M. *The Falls of St. Anthony: The Waterfall that Built Minneapolis*. St. Paul: MHS Press, 1987.

What's in a Name? Snelling
MHS. "History Topics: Josiah Snelling." See http://www.mnhs.org/library/tips/history_topics/127josiah_snelling.htm (December 19, 2008)
Wikipedia. "Josiah Snelling." See http://en.wikipedia.org/wiki/Josiah_Snelling (December 19, 2008).
———. "Fort Snelling, Minnesota." See http://en.wikipedia.org/wiki/Fort_St._Anthony (December 19, 2008).
Hall, Steve. *Fort Snelling: Colossus of the Wilderness*. St. Paul: MHS Press, 1987.

Early Settlement Life
Kane, Lucile M. *The Falls of St. Anthony: The Waterfall that Built Minneapolis*. St. Paul: MHS Press, 1987.
Morris, Lucy Leavenworth Wilder, ed. *Old Rail Fence Corners: Frontier Tales Told by Minnesota Pioneers*. St. Paul: MHS Press, 1914 (1976 reprint). Quote from "Mrs. James Pratt—1850," pp. 52–54.

Keith
National Archives. *General Land Entry File Affidavit, Henry C. Keith*, April 27, 1855.
———. *General Land Entry File Affidavit, Asa Keith*. April 30, 1855.
Merrill, Mary Addie Keith. *Memory*. Minneapolis: N.p., 1933. Pamphlet available at MHS, St. Paul.
Agricultural Census of the United States—1860. Richfield Township.
Minnesota State Census, 1857. Old Military Reserve.
See HQO for the following:
   Eighth Census of the United States—1860. Richfield Township.
   Ninth Census of the United States—1870. Minneapolis Township.
   Tenth Census of the United States—1880. Minneapolis Township, 1st District.

Minneapolis City Directories, 1867–1875.
Merrill, Mary Adelaide Keith. *The Keith Book*. Minneapolis: Lund, 1934.

Moulton
National Archives. *General Land Entry File Affidavit, Dorwin Moulton*. April 24, 1855.
Minnesota State Census, 1857. Old Military Reserve.
See HQO for the following:
   Eighth Census of the United States—1860. Richfield Township.
   Ninth Census of the United States—1870. Minneapolis Township.
   Tenth Census of the United States—1880. Minneapolis Township, 1st District.
Portrait and Biographical Record of Winnebago and Boone Counties, Illinois. Chicago: Biographical Publishing, 1892.
"Obituary—Darwin [sic] E. Moulton." Clippings file, Boone County Historical Society and Museum, Belvidere, Illinois.

Falls City
Library of Congress, American Memory. "Today in History: August 24. The Panic of 1857." See http://memory.loc.gov/ammem/today/aug24.html (December 19, 2008)
Moulton and Keith advertisement. *Minnesota Republican*, August 13, 1857.
"An Act to Incorporate the Mississippi River Improvement and Manufacturing Company." *Minnesota Territorial Laws, 1857*. (Chapter LVIII [58], p. 230.)
National Archives. *General Land Entry File Affidavit, Henry C. Keith*. April 27, 1855.
———. *General Land Entry File Affidavit, Dorwin Moulton*, April 24, 1855.
Falls City steamboat ad. *St. Anthony Express*, June 16, 1855.
"The 'Falls City.'" *St. Anthony Express*, July 14, 1855
Morris, Lucy Leavenworth Wilder, ed. *Old Rail Fence Corners: Frontier Tales Told by Minnesota Pioneers*. St. Paul: MHS Press, 1914 (1976 reprint).

Writers' Program of the Work Projects Administration in the State of Minnesota. *Minneapolis: The Story of a City*. N.p.: Minnesota Writers Project, WPA, 1940.

What's in a Name? Dorman
Carothers, Neil. *Fractional Money: A History of the Small Coins and Fractional Paper Currency of the United States*. New York: Wiley and Sons, 1930.
Minneapolis City Directories, 1867–1905.

Wass Sisters
National Archives. *General Land Entry File Affidavit, John Wass*, April 23, 1855.
Minnesota State Census, 1857. Richfield Township.
Agricultural Census of the United States—1860. Richfield Township.
See HQO for the following:
   Eighth Census of the United States—1860. Richfield Township.
   Ninth Census of the United States—1870. Hot Springs Township, Napa County, California.
   Tenth Census of the United States—1880. Minneapolis.
   Twelfth Census of the United States—1900. 11th Ward, Minneapolis.
   Thirteenth Census of the United States—1910. Los Angeles Township, Precinct 13, Los Angeles.
   Fourteenth Census of the United States—1920. Hollenbeck Home, Los Angeles Township, Los Angeles.
Minneapolis City Directories, 1867–1909.
Minnesota State Medical Examining Board. *Official Register of Physicians*. St. Paul: The board, 1883–1890 editions.
Northwestern University, Woman's Medical School. *Woman's Medical School, Northwestern University (Woman's Medical College of Chicago): The Institution and Its Founders, Class Histories 1870–1896*. Chicago: H. G. Cutler, 1896.
Polk's Medical Register and Directory of North America. Detroit: Polk, 1906, 1908, and 1910 editions.

Wass, Lizzie R., to Henry L. Wills, Northwestern University Foundation, June 15, 1932. Available at Northwestern University Archives, Chicago.

State of California Death Certificate for Anness T. Wass, January 17, 1917.

State of California Death Certificate for Lizzie Rebecca Wass, September 23, 1937.

Chapter 3: Longfellow in 1900

E. F. Griswold Pickling Company ad. *Minneapolis City Directory*, *1898*, p. 1465.

Twelfth Census of the United States–1900. 12th Ward Minneapolis. HQO.

Sanborn Map Company. *Insurance Maps of Minneapolis*. New York: The author, 1912, p. 413.

Residential Life in 1900
Minneapolis City Directories, 1882–1896.

Libby Family
See HQO for the following:
Twelfth Census of the United States– 1900. 12th Ward Minneapolis.
Thirteenth Census of the United States– 1910. 12th Ward Minneapolis.
Minneapolis City Directories, 1880–1920.
"B. J. Libby, Veteran Fuel Dealer, Dies: Minneapolis Pioneer Lived in Same Ward since Birth in March, 1867." *MJ*, October 21, 1920, p. 11.
Sanborn Map Company. *Insurance Maps of Minneapolis*. New York: The author, 1912, p. 440.
"Obituary, Mrs. Hannah J. Libby." *MJ*, May 29, 1902, p. 6.
"Aged Pioneer is Dead: Allen D. Libby Had Lived in Same House for Forty Years." *MJ*, July 18, 1911.

Longfellow School
Zellie, Carol. *Minneapolis Public Schools Historic Context Study*. Minneapolis: Minneapolis Heritage Preservation Commission, 2005.
Minneapolis City Directories, 1885/1886–1911.
"Kindergarten Progress in Minneapolis." *MJ*, February 4, 1899, Part 2, p. 5.

Forman, Robert, and Ruth Forman. "The Longfellow School Story." *Hennepin County History* (Winter 1960): 3.

Fire Station
Firefighters Hall and Museum. "The Fire Alarm Telegraph." *See* http://www.fire-hallmuseum.org/ (December 6, 2008).
Extra Alarm Association of the Twin Cities. "Fire Alarm Telegraph—St. Paul and Minneapolis." *See* http://www.extraalarm.org/fat_main.htm (December 6, 2008).
"Gamewell Fire Alarm Telegraph Register." *See* http://uv201.com/Misc_Pages/gamewell.htm (December 11, 2008).
Virtual Museum of the City of San Francisco. "City Lightning: How the Fire Alarm Telegraph Is Worked." *San Francisco Daily Chronicle*, February 11, 1877. *See* http://www.sfmuseum.org/sffd/alarm.html (January 3, 2009).
Forgotten NY—Street Scenes. "Fire Alarms." *See* http://www.forgotten-ny.com/STREETSCENES/Fire Alarms page/Alarms.html (January 3, 2009).
Sanborn Map Company. *Insurance Maps of Minneapolis*. New York: The author, 1912, p. 439.
Fire Alarm Box locations, *Minneapolis City Directory*, *1900*, pp. 49–52.
Patrick's Cabaret. "About the Building." *See* http://www.patrickscabaret.org/about/building.shtml (December 11, 2008).

Lauritzen Blacksmith Shop
Minneapolis City Directories, 1888/89–1901 and 1927–1962.
See HQO for the following:
Twelfth Census of the United States– 1900. 12th Ward Minneapolis.
Thirteenth Census of the United States– 1910. 12th Ward Minneapolis.
Fourteenth Census of the United States – 1920. 12th Ward Minneapolis.
Wilkins, Craig. "A Small Bit of the Past." *LM*, April 1985, p. 1.
Southtown Personalities: As Interviewed by Don Rivers, Miss Audrey Lewis and Gordon Daline, and Published in The East Lake Shopper, 1934–35. Minneapolis: American, 1936.

Dairyland
See HQO for the following:
Tenth Census of the United States– 1880. Minneapolis Township, 1st District.
Twelfth Census of the United States– 1900. 12th Ward Minneapolis.
Thirteenth Census of the United States– 1910. 12th Ward Minneapolis.
History of Hennepin County and the City of Minneapolis. Minneapolis: North Star, 1881.
USDA National Agricultural Statistics Service—Quick Stats. "Minnesota Data—Dairy, 2006–07." *See* http://www.nass.usda.gov/QuickStats/ (December 6, 2008).
Bratt, Carola. "Longfellow Neighbors, Victor Nelson: Minnehaha Dairy." *LNM*, January 1988, p. 3.
Minnesota State Dairy and Food Commissioner. *Fifth Biennial Report of the Minnesota State Dairy and Food Commissioner*. St. Paul: Pioneer Press, 1894.
———. *Tenth Biennial Report of the Minnesota State Dairy and Food Commissioner*. St. Paul: Pioneer Press, 1904.
Minneapolis City Directories, 1890/91–1916.
Atwater and Flandreau lease to Aaron Johansson for a dairy farm, 1897. Hennepin County Property Records. *Miscellaneous Book 76*: 183.
DuPuis, E. Melanie. *Nature's Perfect Food: How Milk Became America's Drink*. New York: New York University Press, 2002.
Minnesota State Census—1905. 12th Ward, Minneapolis. MHS.

Slumlord of 27½ Street
Foreman, Carolyn Thomas. "General Eli Lundy Huggins." *Chronicles of Oklahoma* 13 (no. 3, September 1935): 255–65.
Home of Heroes. "Photo of Grave Site of MOH Recipient Eli Lundy Huggins." *See* http://64.70.201.125/gravesites/states/ pages_go/huggins_eli_ca.html (November 30, 2008).
Minneapolis City Directories, 1872–1926.

Chapter 4: Social Life

Nordstrom, Gerald T. *Where Youth Meets Truth: A History of Minnehaha Academy*. Minneapolis: Minnehaha Academy, 2001.

See HQO for the following:
Thirteenth Census of the United States– 1910. 12th Ward Minneapolis.
Fourteenth Census of the United States—1920. 12th Ward Minneapolis.
Fifteenth Census of the United State– 1930. 12th Ward Minneapolis.
Boettcher, Nick. *Longfellow Community Population and Housing Characteristics, 1940–2000: An Analysis of the Census Data*. Minneapolis: University of Minnesota, Center for Urban and Regional Affairs, 2006. *See* http://www.cura.umn.edu/publications/NPCR-reports/npcr1265.pdf (December 8, 2008).
Hobbs, Frank, and Nicole Stoops. *Census 2000 Special Reports, Series CENSR-4, Demographic Trends in the 20th Century*. Washington: U.S. Government Printing Office, 2002.

Danish Young People's Home
Danish American Center. "Danish Young People/s Home, 1918–1966." *See* http://www.daf-mn.org/ (December 5, 2008).

Danebo
Danish American Center. "History of Danebo from 1924–1974." *See* http://www.daf-mn.org/ (December 5, 2008).
Danish American Center. "Memory Circle: A Memory Circle at Danebo, 2-18-2005." *See* http://www.daf-mn.org/ (December 5, 2008).
Nathanson, Iric. "Danebo Home Shuts Down Senior Housing." *LNM*, April 2005.

Snelling Avenue African-American Community
Taylor, David Vassar. *African Americans in Minnesota*. St. Paul: MHS Press, 2002.

See HQO for the following:
> *Thirteenth Census of the United States—1910.* 12th Ward Minneapolis.
> *Fourteenth Census of the United States—1920.* 12th Ward Minneapolis.
> *Fifteenth Census of the United States—1930.* 12th Ward Minneapolis.

"Sylvestus Phelps Williams, Here 35 Years, Dies." *Minneapolis Spokesman*, November 10, 1944, p. 1.

Minneapolis City Directories, 1915–1929.

Michael J. Dowling School

Faries, John Culbert. "Michael J. Dowling," c. 1943. In *Michael J. and Jennie B. Dowling Papers, 1883–1944*, on microfilm, MHS, St. Paul.

"A Tribute to a Great Minneapolitan—Michael J. Dowling: 1866–1921." *Hennepin County History* (Summer 1967): 9.

Nathanson, Iric. "School of Choice." *Hennepin History* (Winter 1996): 22–32

Lutheran Children's Friend Society

"Dr. Glabe to Be Honored on His Retirement." *Lutheran Children's Friend* 47 (no. 5, September–October 1968): 2.

Mindrum, Beverly. "Adoption Unit to Give Families Living Dolls for Christmas." *Minneapolis Star*, December 13, 1962. In "Lutheran Children's Friend Society" clippings file, Special Collections, MCL.

"Children's Agency has Busy Year." *Minneapolis Star*, March 14, 1964. In "Lutheran Children's Friend Society" clippings file, Special Collections, MCL.

Offermann, Glenn W. *Missouri in Minnesota: A Centennial History of the Minnesota South District, Lutheran Church—Missouri Synod, 1882–1982*. N.p.: The district, 1982.

Sheltering Arms

Davenport, Florence Bodley. *A Brief History of the Sheltering Arms of the Diocese of Minnesota, 1882–1922* (pamphlet). Minneapolis: Sheltering Arms, 1922. MHS.

The Sheltering Arms: 101 Years of Caring: A Look at the Years 1882–1983 and Beyond. Minneapolis: Bolger, 1983.

"Sheltering Arms to be Converted into Sister Kenny Polio Hospital." *MSJ*, August 23, 1942, p. L1.

"Sheltering Arms Neighbors Oppose Polio Hospital Plan." *MSJ*, September 29, 1942. In "Sheltering Arms" clippings file, Special Collections, MCL.

"Council Refers Polio Clinic Row to Committee." *MSJ*, October 9, 1942. In "Sheltering Arms" clippings file, Special Collections, MCL.

"Sue to Bar Hospital at Sheltering Arms." *MSJ*, March 24, 1943. In "Sheltering Arms" clippings file, Special Collections, MCL.

Corner Store

Chase, Fern. *A Study of Community Conditions: South District*. Minneapolis: Women's Co-Operative Alliance, 1926.

Longfellow grocer and meat business listings compiled and mapped from *Minneapolis City Directories*, 1915, 1925, 1935, 1950.

Improvement Associations

Hiawatha

"Hiawatha Improvement Association Has Built Its Own Clubhouse." *MJ*, October 25, 1908, p. 10.

"Does Much for Its Locality: Hiawatha Improvement Association Points with Pride to Two Years History." *MJ*, May 10, 1910, section 2, p. 10.

"Hiawatha Improvement Association Wants Home of Its Own." *MJ*, July 3, 1908, p. 7.

Other articles on the Hiawatha Improvement Association appeared in the *MJ*: July 22, 1908 (p. 6), September 9, 1908 (p. 7), November 11, 1908 (p. 6), and November 18, 1908 (p. 5).

Thirteenth Census of the United State—1910. 12th Ward Minneapolis. HQO.

Sanborn Map Company. *Insurance Maps of Minneapolis*. New York: The author, 1912, p. 549.

Minneapolis City Directories, 1908–1930.

Chase, Fern. *A Study of Community Conditions: South District*. Minneapolis: Women's Co-Operative Alliance, 1926.

Seven Oaks

Longfellow plats (subdivisions). Hennepin County Recorders Office.

Thirteenth Census of the United State—1910. 12th Ward Minneapolis. HQO.

Minneapolis City Directories, 1908–1915.

"Seven Oaks Men Meet." *MJ*, April 14, 1908, p. 6.

"Know What They Want: Seven Oaks Residents Will Work for All Public Improvements." *MJ*, May 12, 1908, p. 13.

"Neighborhood Union for Residents of Seven Oaks." *Minneapolis Labor Review* (October 18, 1912): 4.

Minneapolis Public Schools, Architectural Division. "Minneapolis Public Schools, 1851–2000: A History of Past and Present Schools and Sites Showing Tenure of Site Ownership, Duration of Enrollment, School Building Construction" (poster-sized graph). Minneapolis: The author, June 1985.

Chapter 5: Entertainment

Minnehaha Driving Park

Wikipedia. "Harness Racing." *See* http://en.wikipedia.org/wiki/Harness_racing (December 21, 2008).

Brady, Tim. *The Great Dan Patch and the Remarkable Mr. Savage*. Minneapolis: Nodin, 2006.

"Being Rushed Through." *St. Paul Daily Globe*, May 20, 1888, p. 9.

Available at the Harness Racing Museum and Hall of Fame, Goshen, NY:
Clark's Horse Review, July 11, 1893, p. 1295.
The Horse Review, July 9, 1901, p. 750.
The Horse Review, July 8, 1902, p. 716.

Diers, John W., and Aaron Isaacs. *Twin Cities by Trolley: The Streetcar Era in Minneapolis and St. Paul*. Minneapolis: University of Minnesota Press, 2007.

"Road Runner Parade: One Will Signalize Opening of Minnehaha Track." *MJ*, May 21, 1901, p. 12.

"Old Track Renewed." *MJ*, May 27, 1901, p. 9.

"'Haha Track Is No More: Once Famous Race Course Will Be Cut Up into Building Lots." *MJ*, March 28, 1903, p. 24.

Zalusky, Joseph W. "'Fish' Jones and His Irresistible Longfellow Gardens." *Hennepin County History* (Fall 1967): 7.

Foote, C. M. *Atlas of the City of Minneapolis, Minnesota*. Minneapolis: C. M. Foote, 1892, plates 49, 50.

Minneapolis Millers Baseball

Thornley, Stew. "Nicollet Park." *See* http://stewthornley.net/nicollet_park.html (December 21, 2008).

———. *Baseball in Minnesota: The Definitive History*. St. Paul: MHS Press, 2006.

"Duluth Gets Another Drubbing." *Omaha Daily Bee*, July 20, 1891, p. 2.

Minnehaha Park

Anfinson, John O. *River of History: A Historic Resources Study of Mississippi National River and Recreation Area*. St. Paul: Corps, St. Paul District, 2003. *See also* http://www.nps.gov/miss/historyculture/ ("Historic Resources Study").

Wikipedia. "Minnehaha Falls." *See* http://en.wikipedia.org/wiki/Minnehaha_Falls (December 27, 2008).

Petersen, William J. *Steamboating on the Upper Mississippi*. New York: Dover, 1995 (originally published 1937).

Longfellow, Henry Wadsworth. *The Poems of Henry Wadsworth Longfellow*. New York: Thomas Y. Crowell, 1901.

Hallberg, Jane King. *Minnehaha Creek—Living Waters*. Minneapolis: Cityscapes, 1988.

Zalusky, Joseph W. "'Fish' Jones and his Irresistible Longfellow Gardens." *Hennepin County History* (Fall 1967): 7.

Minneapolis Park and Recreation Board. *The Story of WPA and Other Federal Aid Projects in the Minneapolis Parks, Parkways and Playgrounds*. Minneapolis: The board, 1937.

———. *The Minnehaha Park Renovation Plan*. Minneapolis: The board, 1992.

Wonderland Park

"Big Force of Men Hustling at the Wonderland Park." *MJ*, May 18, 1905, p. 7.

"Crowds at Wonderland." *MJ*, July 18, 1911, p. 9.

"New and Varied Thrills to Be on Tap in 'Wonderland.'" *MJ*, May 13, 1905, p. 13.

Wold, James T. "Wonderland Amusement Park Was the Greatest of Its Time." *Southside Pride*, August 1995, p. 12.

"The Wonderful Fairy Theater—Audiences See it thru Lenses." *MJ*, May 27, 1905, p. 14.

British Columbia Adventure Network. "Chilkoot Trail: The Route to the Klondike Gold Rush." See http://www.bcadventure.com/adventure/explore/north/trails/chilkoot.htm (December 21, 2008).

Lieberman, Hannah. "Incubator Baby Shows: A Medical and Social Frontier." *The History Teacher* 35 (no. 1, November 2001): 81–88.

Nathanson, Iric. "Wonderland Amusement Park Operated Like Proper Resort for Ladies, Children." *LNM*, September 2005.

Rascher Insurance Map Publishing Company. *Atlas of Minneapolis and Suburbs, Minnesota*. Chicago: The author, 1905–06, plate 308.

Lee, Betty. "Wonderland Didn't Last Long." *LM*, September 1984, p. 4.

Movie Theaters

Besse, Kirk J. *Show Houses: Twin Cities Style*. Minneapolis: Victoria, 1997.

Minneapolis Public Library. "Theaters." See http://www.mpls.lib.mn.us/history/ae2.asp (February 3, 2008).

Kenney, Dave. *Twin Cities Picture Show: A Century of Moviegoing*. St. Paul: MHS Press, 2007.

Sanborn Map Company. *Insurance Maps of Minneapolis*. New York: The author, 1912, p. 440.

Chase, Fern. *A Study of Community Conditions: South District*. Minneapolis: Women's Co-operative Alliance, 1926.

City of Minneapolis, Heritage Preservation Commission. *National Register of Historic Places—Nomination Form*. See http://www.ci.minneapolis.mn.us/hpc/landmarks/Lake_St_E_3500-06_El_Largo_Theater.asp (December 21, 2008). (Original form published December 1982.)

Lee, Betty. "The Historic El Lago Theater [sic]." *LM*, September 1985, p. 13.

Talking Motion Pictures. "A Brief History of Talking Pictures." See http://xroads.virginia.edu/~UG00/3on1/movies/talkies.html (December 21, 2008).

Minneapolis City Directories, 1927–1983.

"Local Elders Remember the El Lago Theater." *LM*, October 1985, p. 10.

"C.L.U. Warned of More Pay Cut Moves." *Minneapolis Labor Review*, January 29, 1932, p. 5.

"Falls Theatre Has Phoney Union Sign." *Minneapolis Labor Review*, April 1, 1932, p. 1.

"The Tarnished Silver Screen, or Whither Neighborhood Theatres?" *The Villager*, May 11, 1977, p. 20.

"New Theater Draws National Attention." *Minneapolis Tribune*, March 13, 1949, p. G16.

"Dream Homes Have Nothing on Theaters." *Minneapolis Star*, April 14, 1956, p. 14A.

"Volk Bros. Spend $50,000 Renovating Riverview Theatre [sic] at Minneapolis." *Box Office* (March 31, 1956).

"New Beauty for an 'Almost New' House." *Box Office* (June 8, 1957).

"Modernized, Partly to Get Free Flow throughout the Interior." *Motion Picture Herald*, July 7, 1956, p. 10.

Riverview Theater. "History." See http://www.riverviewtheater.com/about/ (December 13, 2008).

Cinema Treasures. "Riverview Theater." See http://cinematreasures.org/theater/802/ (December 13, 2008).

Chapter 6: The Building of Longfellow

Infrastructure

For sewer and water-main maps, see "Annual Report of the Minneapolis City Engineer." In *Annual Reports of the Various City Officers of the City of Minneapolis*. Minneapolis: The city, 1895, 1897, 1898, 1907, 1908, 1909, 1910, 1911, 1912, and 1913.

Arnott, Sigrid. "Twin Cities Sanitation History" January 1996. See http://www.fromsitetostory.org/sources/papers/tcmsanitation/tcmsanitation.asp (December 28, 2008).

Minnesota Rural Drinking Water Association. "Key Dates in the History of the Minnesota Drinking Water Program." See http://www.mrwa.com/waterkey-dates.htm (December 28, 2008).

Wisdom, Joyce. "Lake Street History Tells the Story of Our Great Street." *The Lake Line* (Spring 2007): 2.

City of Minneapolis, On the Agenda: City of Minneapolis Actions & Issues October 3, 1997. "Paving Crews Lay Final Section of 605-Mile Residential Street Paving Program." See http://www.ci.minneapolis.mn.us/news/publications/ (December 31, 2008).

"Street Paving Project for Summer of '83." *LM*, March 1983, p. 11.

Streetcar

Diers, John W., and Aaron Isaacs. *Twin Cities by Trolley: The Streetcar Era in Minneapolis and St. Paul*. Minneapolis: University of Minnesota Press, 2007.

Metro Transit. "Route 7, " "Route 21," "Route 24." See http://www.metrotransit.org/ (December 31, 2008).

Housing Styles

McAlester, Virginia, and Lee McAlester. *A Field Guide to American Houses*. Mount Vernon, NY: Consumers Union, 1984.

Dates of construction: City of Minneapolis property information (GIS) data for the years cited; Longfellow-specific data from Longfellow Community Council.

Longfellow subdivision (plat) data compiled by Eric Hart from original plat records at the Hennepin County Public Records Division, Minneapolis.

Sears Archive. "What Is a Sears Modern Home?" See http://www.searsarchives.com/homes/ (January 11, 2009).

"Sevenoaks." *Walton's Home Builder*, June 1915.

Edmund G. Walton Agency. *Homes in the Making*. Minneapolis: The agency, c. 1910. Pamphlet available at MHS, St. Paul.

Public Schools

Minneapolis Public Schools, Architectural Division. "Minneapolis Public Schools, 1851–2000: A History of Past and Present Schools and Sites Showing Tenure of Site Ownership, Duration of Enrollment, School Building Construction" (poster-size graph). Minneapolis: The author, June 1985.

"Old School—New Use." *LM*, August 1985, p. 1.

Milbraith, Bill. "Old Simmons School—New Minnehaha Manor." *LM*, November 1985, p. 4.

———. "Who was Henry M. Simmons?" *LM*, May 1986, p. 2.

———. "Longfellow—A Rich History" (handout from Longfellow's Wonderland Festival, September 14, 1986). Available at Hennepin History Museum Archives, Minneapolis.

Zellie, Carole. *Minneapolis Public Schools Historic Context Study*. St. Paul: Landscape Research LLC, 2005.

Minneapolis Public Schools. "History of Minneapolis Public Schools—Howe." See https://secure.mpls.k12.mn.us/mpsHistory/facility.aspx?facility=51&name=Howe (January 26, 2009).

Minneapolis Harvester Works

Neill, Edward D. *History of Hennepin County and the City of Minneapolis*. Minneapolis: North Star, 1881, p. 411.

Sanborn Map Company. *Insurance Maps of Minneapolis*. New York: The author, 1885, p. 34.

"Old Harvester Works Go." *MJ*, November 19, 1900, p. 6.

MSMC and Minneapolis-Moline

Thomas, Norman F. *Minneapolis-Moline: A History of Its Formation and Operations*. Unpublished thesis, University of Minnesota, 1953.

Wold, James T. "Moline Has Long History in South Minneapolis." *Southside Pride* (March 1995): 13.

"To Labor Papers in Other Cities: Introducing George M. Gillette." *Minneapolis Labor Review*. July 14, 1916, p. 1.

"Women at Steel and Machinery Shop Learn New Working Vocabulary." *Minneapolis Tribune*, November 3, 1918, pp. B11.

Sanborn Map Company. *Insurance Maps of Minneapolis*. New York: The author, 1951, pp. 412–13.

Grain Elevators

Minneapolis City Directories, 1885–1970.

Sanborn Map Company. *Insurance Maps of Minneapolis*. New York: The author, 1912, pp. 466, 486, 507, 541.

—. *Insurance Maps of Minneapolis.* New York: The author, 1951, pp. 466, 486, 506, 507, 1013.

Frame, Robert M., III. *Grain Elevators in Minnesota.* St. Paul: MHS, State Historic Preservation Office, 1989.

"Coming Down." *Minneapolis Star,* July 23, 1974.

Wagner, Bill. "Quigley Family, Grain Coop Share History with Longfellow/Nokomis Community." *LNM,* September 1992, p. 16.

MHS. "Grain Terminal Association: An Inventory of Its Corporate Records at the MHS." *See* http://www.mnhs.org/library/findaids/00492.html (July 6, 2008).

Mills

Sanborn Map Company. *Insurance Maps of Minneapolis.* New York: The author, 1951, pp. 486, 507.

"Local Milling Co. Announces New Product Containing Vitamin D." *East Lake Shopper,* March 21, 1935, p. 7.

Chapter 7: Longfellow in the 21st Century

Nathanson, Iric. "Longfellow Nokomis Property Values Soar." *LNM,* May 2000.

The Rise and Fall of the Resource Center of the Americas

Nathanson, Iric. "Developer Goes to Work on Coliseum Building." *LNM,* February 2000.

North, Ryan. "Resource Center Suspends Operations." *LNM,* September 2007, p. 1.

Turck, Mary. "Resource Center of the Americas Closes after 24 Years." *Twin Cities Planet. See* http://tcdailyplanet.net/ (December 8, 2008).

Resource Center of the Americas. "Mosaic of the Americas." *See* http://www.americas.org/mosaicoftheamericas (December 8, 2008).

The End of the Working Man's Bar

Stratton, Jeremy. "Poodle Gets the Irish Blues." *The Bridge* (November 2007): 10.

Mauer, Karolyn. "Longfellow and Nokomis Bars, Restaurants Grapple with New Smoking Ban." *LNM,* June 2005, p. 3.

Willms, Jan. "Some Longfellow Nokomis Businesses Faltering under Minneapolis Smoking Ban." *LNM,* September 2005, p. 3.

Lake Street Reconstruction

For general information on Lake Street Reconstruction, *see* http://www.lakestreet.info/planning/future.php (December 9, 2008).

Diers, John W., and Aaron Isaacs. *Twin Cities by Trolley: The Streetcar Era in Minneapolis and St. Paul.* Minneapolis: University of Minnesota Press, 2007.

Anders, Elizabeth. "Lake Street PAC Votes to Explore Three-Lane Options East of Hiawatha." *LNM,* January 2004, p. 6.

The Midtown Greenway

For background on the Midtown Greenway, *see* http://www.midtowngreenway.org/trailusers/ (December 9, 2008)

Hart, Eric. "Midtown Greenway Coming to Longfellow." *LNM,* March 2001, p. 18.

Nathanson, Iric. "Midtown Greenway Enthusiasts Await Dramatic Suspension Bridge." *LNM,* May 2005, p. 13.

LRT and Highway 55

"Stop Highway 55 Reroute, November 1999." *See* http://treaty.indigenousnative.org/highway7_nov.html (December 10, 2008).

Faces of Resistance, Gallery 7. "Highway 55." *See* http://www.cpinternet.com/~mbayly/facesofresistance7.htm (December 10, 2008).

For background on light rail, *see* http://www.metrotransit.org/rail/facts.asp (December 9, 2008).

Metropolitan Council. *Hiawatha Light-Rail Transit Facts,* (Pub. 14-08-041) July 2008. *See* also http://www.metrocouncil.org/about/facts/HiawathaLRTFacts.pdf (November 26, 2008).

Rain Gardens

Elsen, Rachel. "Business Owners React to Stormwater Management Fees." *LNM,* April 2005, p. 6.

—. "Longfellow Moves to Curb Stormwater Runoff." *LNM,* February 2005, p. 2.

Brotz, Deborah. "Beautiful Rain Garden Replaces Drab Fence and Blacktop at Sanford Middle School." *LNM,* September 2006, p. 16.

Metro Produce

"No Idlers Allowed." *Minneapolis Observer* (February 3, 2005). *See* http://www.mplsobserver.com/node /64 (December 9, 2008).

North, Ryan. "Federal Court OKs Metro Produce's Ability to Operate Trucks at Night." *LNM,* March 2007, p. 6.

—. "Metro Produce, City of Minneapolis Settle over Noise Dispute." *LNM,* April 2007, p. 3.

Building Boom

Nathanson, Iric. "West River Commons Project to Rebuild in Wake of Tragic Fire." *LNM,* August 2003, p. 1.

City of Minneapolis, Community Planning and Economic Development. "Hiawatha Commons." See http://www.ci.minneapolis.mn.us/cped/hiawatha_commons.asp (December 9, 2008).

Nathanson, Iric. "Hiawatha Commons Tenants Find New Home at Affordable Rents." *LNM,* February 2007, p. 16.

Willms, Jan. "Longfellow Community Negotiating Agreement with Purina Site Developer." *LNM,* February 2007, p. 10.

—. "Developer and Community Closer to Agreement on Purina Project." *LNM,* March 2008, p. 1.

North, Ryan. "Construction Project on 46th and 46th Comes to a Halt." *LNM,* September 2006, p. 11.

ILLUSTRATION CREDITS

Courtesy of the Minnesota Historical Society: pp. i (A. F. Raymond), ii *(Minneapolis Journal)*, 1, 5 (Henry Lewis), 7 (Benjamin Franklin Upton), 8, 9 both, 10 top (Smith), 11–12 all, 13 middle (J. E. Quigley), 13 bottom (Norton & Peel), 17–18 (Tallmadge Elwell), 20 and 21 bottom (Benjamin Franklin Upton), 21 top, 23 (Benjamin Franklin Upton), 29 and 32 (Charles J. Hibbard), 36 (A. F. Raymond), 40, 43, 44 (Norton & Peel), 45, 46 top, 48, 49, 51 middle, 51 bottom (Lee Brothers), 53 top, 54 both, 57 top (Hibbard Studio), 57 bottom (Norton & Peel), 61, 67, 68, 70 both, 71 both (top Robert Mauritz Swenson), 72, 77, 78, 80, 81 (Norton & Peel), 87 top *(Minneapolis Journal)*, 87 bottom (Norton & Peel), 88 (George E. Luxton), 89 bottom, 90 top, 91, 92 bottom, 93 top (Arthur H. Jensen), 95 (Charles J. Hibbard), 96 and 97 (Norton & Peel), 98 bottom (Charles J. Hibbard), 99 top (Hibbard Studio), 99 bottom and 100 (Norton & Peel)

Cindy Craig Harper map: p. viii

Collection of Eric Hart: pp. 3, 31, 39

Courtesy of the Mississippi National River and Recreation Area: pp. 6 both, 15, 16 both, 109 both, 114 bottom

Eric Hart photos: pp. 8 bottom, 13 top, 33 all, 38 both, 56 all, 59, 60 bottom, 76 top, 85, 86 bottom, 102, 104 both, 108 both, 111–13 all

Courtesy of the Collections of the Hennepin History Museum: pp. 27 top, 62, 63 bottom, 73, 74 bottom, 84 both, 86 top, 90 bottom, 93 bottom

Courtesy of the Drexel University College of Medicine, Archives and Special Collections on Women in Medicine and Homeopathy: p. 27 both bottom

Courtesy of the Hennepin County Library, James K. Hosmer Special Collections Library, Minneapolis Collection: pp. 34 (M1585), 35 (M1816)

Courtesy of the Danish American Center: pp. 46 both, 47 both

Works Progress Administration: pp. 52, 53 bottom, 94

Courtesy of the Minneapolis Central Labor Union Council, AFL-CIO: pp. 60 top, 75, 92 top

Courtesy of the Riverview Theater: pp. 63 top, 76 bottom

Courtesy of The Harness Racing Museum and Hall of Fame, Goshen, New York: p. 64

Bill Lundborg photos: pp. 74 top, 101

Courtesy of the Minnesota Streetcar Museum: pp. 82, 83 (William Janssen)

Terry Faust photos: 103, 106, 107

Hillary Oppmann photos: 110 both

Charles Bowler photo: 114 top

INDEX

Page references in italics indicate pages including illustrations.

Except as noted, street entries are east and avenues are south.

1st Avenue North, 25
12th Ward, ix, 55
16th-century Italian style, 74
18th Street, 49
19th century, x, 2, 38, 49, 88
20th century, ix, 2, 5, 15, 30, 32–33, 38, 40, 44–45, 49, 59, 63, 65, 78, 81, 84–85, 102, 105
21st century, x, 47, 58, *102*, 105, 107, 109, 112
24th Street, 10, 26, 28
25th Street, 73
26th Avenue, 28, *35*, 94
26th Street, 25, 27, 39
27th Avenue, 44, 58, 72–73, 78–79, 81, 107–08, 111; 3012 27th, *107*
27th Street, ix, 4, 12, 15, 26, 30, 32–33, 41–42, 104
27½ Street, 41–42
28th Avenue, 33, 41, *104*, 111, 113; 2800 28th, *33*; 3107 28th, *33*, 34
28th Street, 8, 21, 25, 38–39, 41, 84, 88–89, 92, *94*, 111
29th Avenue, (2841), *33*
29th Street, *30*, 35, 89
2nd US Calvary, 41
30th Avenue, 70
31st Avenue, 22, 25, 35, *38*, 39, *56–57*, 69, 72, 82, 86; 3301 31st, *56*, 57
31st Street, 33–35, *38*, 39, 60, 72, 86–87, 103; 2801 31st, *38*; 3101–11 31st, 72; 3320 31st, *38*
32nd Avenue, 39, 69
32nd Street, 60, 69, 87
33rd Avenue, 26, 69
33rd Street, 70, 88, 95, 108
34th Avenue, 4, 30, 38–39, *84*
34th Street, 22, 27, 48, 59, *81*, 95, 113
35th Avenue, 59, 84
35th Street, *15*, 95, *96*, 98, 106
36th Avenue, 81–82, *83*, 84
36th Street, *3*, *16*, 48, 51, *52*, 63, *65*, 88
37th Avenue, 60, *81*, 87
37th Street, 63–64, *80*, 84, 99
38th Avenue, 4, 25–27, 38, 60, *87*; 3100 38th, *87*; 3149 38th, *60*
38th Street, 3, *14*, 22, 37, *39*, 40, 53, 58–59, 75, *79*, 80, 87–88, 98–99, *106*, 113
39th Avenue (3408), *110*
39th Street, 48
40th Avenue, 88, 108
40th Street, 73, 81, 85
41st Avenue, 39
41st Street, 82, 95–96, *97*, 98
42nd Avenue, 22, 39, *56–57*, 59, 63, 75, 82, *86*, 88; 3104 42nd, *86*; 3800 42nd, *63*, 75–76; 3957–59 42nd, *56–57*
42nd Street, *3*, 44, 46, 53, 58–59, 81, 85, 88, 106, 113; 3620 42nd, 44, *45–47*, *46*
42nd Street Lofts, 113
43rd Avenue, *85*, 88, 108; 3216 43rd, *85*
43rd Street, 53
44th Avenue, 40, *86*, 88; 3520 44th, *86*
44th Street, *112*, 113
44th Street, 8, 52–53, 58–59, *82*; 3725 45th, *59*
45th Street (3725), 58–59
46th Avenue, *13*, *14*, 38, 39, 53, 81, 82, 85, 112–13
46th Street Hiawatha Light Rail station, 82
46th Street, *13*, *14*, 27, *52*, 113
48th Street (Godfrey Road), 38, *39*–40
4th of July, 64
7-SIGMA, *110*

Abundant Life Christian Center, 74
Aeroplane Ladies, 70
Africa (and African immigrants), 45, 48
African Americans, 45, 48
Airport Taxi, 37
America, 2, 47, 75
American box, 5; Centennial (1776–1876), 34; cinema, 75; milling, 79
Ames, Charles G. (Rev.), 25
Anne Sullivan School, 104
Archer-Daniels-Midland (ADM), 96, 98–99
Arrow-maker (in Longfellow's *The Song of Hiawatha*), 66
Atkinson Milling Company, 99
Atwood, Abby Tuttle, 23
Atwood, Emma, 23
Atwood, Hezekiah, 22
Atwood, Jennie, 23
Australia, 55

Baroque style, 74
Barr Engineering, *110*

Bassett's Creek, 20
"Battle Hymn of the Republic, The," 88
Becketwood, 56
Belvidere (IL), 25
Brackett Park, 102, 104–05
Breck School, 56
Bridge Square, *18*
Brown, Jacob, 66
Brown's Fall (Falls), 4, 66
Bull Tractor Company, 91
Bumping the Bumps, 69
Burlington (IA), 59, 84
Burlington Northern Railroad, 59
Butter-Kist Company, *73*

Cable, Telina, 60
Calhoun's Fall, 4
California, 28
California Plan of school design, 88
Cambridge (MA), 68
Canada, 69
Canadian Pacific Railroad, 104
Capital City Growth, 113
Cargill Elevator T complex, 95–96
Carr, Carolyn, 110–11
Caucasians, 45, 48
Centennial School, *34*
Chain of Lakes, ix, 19, 105
Chicago, 28, 41, 69
Chicago Avenue, 108
Chicago, Burlington & Quincy Railroad, 59, 84
Chicago, Milwaukee, and St. Paul Railway (CM&StP; Milwaukee Road), 95, 98
Chicago, St. Paul and Milwaukee Railroad, 12, 21
Chilkoot Pass, 69
Chinese, 108
Christ Church Lutheran, 51
Christian, 45
Church Memorial Chapel, 54
City of Minneapolis, 67, 105, 111, 113
City of St. Paul, 10
Civil War, 2, 7–8, 12, 25–26, *27*, 41
Clark, William, 19
Clarx Milling Company, 99
Clemens, Samuel L. (Mark Twain), 67
Cleveland, Horace, 6
Close Landscape Architects, 16
CLUES, 108
Coliseum Building, 108

Confer Brothers, *86*
Congress, 3, 8, 10, 22
Congressional Medal of Honor, 41
Cooper, James Fenimore, 88
Cooper Elementary School, *86*, 88
Cooper neighborhood, ix
Corner Store, *56*, 57
Cub Foods, 35, 58, 88, *94*, 108, 113

Dacotah (book by Mary Eastman, 1849), 66
Dairyland, 38
Dakota (Dacotah), the, ix, 18–20, 23, 41, 66, 105, 106; beliefs, 19; warriors, 18
Dakota War of 1862 (Great Sioux Uprising or Dakota Conflict), x, 18, 20, 25, 41
Dan Patch, 64
Danebo ("home of the Danes"), 45, 47
Danebo Old People's Home (3030–3034 West River Parkway), 47
Danish Young People's Home (3620 42nd Street), 44, 45–46, 47
Danish Young People's Home (drawing by Robert James Sorenson), *46*
Davis, Bette, 75
Day School for Mentally Retarded Children, 56
Dayton (MN), 3
Dead Zone (in Gulf of Mexico), 15
Decoration Day, *87*
Denmark (and Danish immigrants), 37–38, 44–47
Devil's Cave, 71
Dight Avenue, 58, 95, *96*–97, 98, 112–13
Dorman Avenue, 27, *113*; 2832 Dorman, 25
Dorman, Anna, 27
Dorman, Dorance, 27
Dorman, Dorlon B., 26–27
Dorman, Mary (later Greer), 27
Dorman's Addition, 27, 38–39
Dorsey, H. A., 69
Dowling, Michael J., 49–50
Dowling Community Garden, *114*
Dupont Avenue, 49, 103

E. F. Griswold Pickling Company, *30*
East 25th Street streetcar line, 13, 82
East African immigrants, 102
East Coast, 69
East Lake Library, 73, 111
East Lake Shopper, 4
East Lake Theater, 72

122 ■ The Neighborhood by the Falls

Eastman, Mary, 66
Ecological Strategies, LLC, 110–11
Edmund Boulevard, *51–52*, 81, 85; 3624 Edmund, 51–52
Edmund G. Walton Agency, 84
El Lago Theatre ("the lake," 3506 Lake Street), *73–74*, *83*
El Norteno (4000 East Lake Street), *108*
El Rodeo nightclub, 108
Elim Presbyterian Church, 69–70
Elite Theater, 72–73
Elk Theater, 72, 74
English language, 108
Episcopal Church Home, 56
Episcopal groups, *48*, 52, 55, 56
Ethiopian, 108
Europe (and Europeans), 14, 48
Eustis, William (Mayor), 50

Falls City (Town of), 2, 18, 25–26, 27; name, 26
Falls of St. Anthony, ix–x, 2, 4, 6–7, 7–10, 14, 18–19, 20–21, 22, 24, 66, 79, 88, 95, 98
Falls Theater (3950–3954 Minnehaha Avenue), 74–75
Farmers Union Elevator, 96–97
Farmers Union Grain Terminal Association (FUGTA or GTA), 96–97
Farmers Union Terminal Association (FUTA), 96
Featherstonhaugh, George, 4
Fifth Avenue, 104
Fire Station Number 21 (3010 Minnehaha Avenue), 21, *36*, 37
Firehouse Theater, 37
Folk (simple vernacular) style, 85
Ford Bridge ("the Intercity"), 7, *11*, *13*, 15, 82
Ford Bridge Drive-In, *13*
Ford Dam (Lock and Dam No. 1), 5
Ford Motor Company, 10; plant, 13, 82
Fort Ripley, 25
Fort St. Anthony, 21
Fort Snelling, x, 4, 7, 8, 18–20, 21–22, 66, 68, 105–06
Fort Snelling (Henry Lewis painting, ca. 1850), *5*
Fort Snelling Road, *22*
Fort Snelling State Park, 19
Franklin Avenue Bridge, 8
Franklin Avenue, 8
Free Will Baptist Church, 25
Friends of the Mississippi River, *109*, 114
Frog Pond, 4

Garden Homes Food Market (3957–59 42nd Avenue), 56–57

Gardner, Orlando N., 33
General Mills, 98
Geological and Natural History Survey of Minnesota, 8
Georgian style, 74
Gillette, George M., 91
Glabe, Edwin Buckley (Rev.), *51–52*
Glacial Lake Agassiz, 6
Glenwood shale, 6
Godfrey mill, 23
Godfrey Road (48th Street), *39*, 40
Government Land Survey map, *22*
Grand Circuit, 64
Grand Rounds trail, 105
Great Western Trotting Circuit, 64
Greek, 108
Griswold, Anna, 30
Griswold, Edward F., 30, *32*
Gulf of Mexico, 15

Ha-Ha Tanka ("big waterfall," Falls of St. Anthony), 19
Hamline Avenue (St. Paul), 63
Hamline University, 41
Harvest States Cooperatives, 97
Harvester Works, 90
Hastings, 3
Health and Hospitals Committee, 55
Hennepin Avenue, 73
Hennepin Avenue Bridge, 25
Hennepin County, 33, 90, 105, 108, 113
Hennepin County Community Welfare Council, 56
Hennepin County Regional Rail Authority, 104
Hersey, Harry, 64
Hiawatha (in Longfellow's *The Song of Hiawatha*), ix, 66–67; Hiawatha and Mudjekeewis, 66; name, ix, 20, 88
Hiawatha Avenue, ix, x 12, *40*, 58, 64, 68, 88, *89*, 92, 95–96, 98–99, *102*, 103–06, 113; 3745 Hiawatha, *99*
Hiawatha Commons, 113
Hiawatha Flats, *112*, 113
Hiawatha Hall (3725 45th Street), 58–59
Hiawatha Improvement Association, *58–59*
Hiawatha Light Rail (LRT) Line, 8, 2l, *106*, 113
Hiawatha neighborhood, ix
Hiawatha Park, 102
Hiawatha School, 59, 86, 88
Hipp, Albert D., 59
Hispanic, 45, 48, 102, 108
Holy Trinity Church, 73, 113
Hopkins, 93

House of Nonsense, *70*
Howe Elementary School, 86, 88
Howe neighborhood, ix
Howe, Julia Ward, 88
Huggins, Alexander G. (Rev.), 41
Huggins, Eli L. (Gen.), *41*

I-35W bridge, *8*
I-94 bridge, 12
Ice Age, 6
Illinois, 93
Improvement Gazetteer, 59
Independent Moving Picture Operators Union, Inc., 75
Indian Fellowship Church, 70
Indian Territory, 41
Indian Wars, 41
Indiana, 44
Indianapolis, 27
Indians (see also Native Americans), 19, 23; missionary, 41; tipis, *18*; trails, 4, 8, 18
Infant Incubator Institute, *71*, 72
Intercity Bridge (Ford Bridge), 13
International Stock Food Company, 64
Iowa, 59, 84
Irish, 108–09

Jack and the Beanstalk, 69
Japanese, 108
Jeep, 92, *93*
Jefferson, Thomas (Pres.), 19
Jeppeson, Charles, 37
Joel, Dale, 113
Johanson, Hans, 38
Johnson School (3100 38th Avenue), *60*, 86–87
Johnson, John A. (Gov.), 87
Johnson, Lyndon B. (Pres.), 67
Johnstown Flood, 69
Jones, Robert F. "Fish," *62*, 63–64, 67–68
June Bride (movie), 75
Keith, Albert, 24
Keith, Asa, 24
Keith, Henry Clay, 24–26
Keith, John, 25
Keith, Mary, 25
Keith, Ruth, 24
Kennedy, John F. (Pres.), 97
Kentucky, 93
Kimball, Hannibal H., 28
Kittsondale track, 63
Klondike Gold Rush, 69

La Clinica en Lake, 108
Lake Amusement Company, 73, 74

Lake Calhoun, 4
Lake Harriet, 4
Lake Minnetonka, 105
Lake Pepin, 14
Lake Street, x, 12, 14, 18, 21, *22*, 25–27, 30, *31*, 33–34, 37–39, 42, 44, 47, 56, 58–59, *62*, 65, 69, *71*, 72–73, 78–83, *84*, 86, 92–94, *102–03*, 104–05, 107–08, 112–13; 2707 Lake, 72, 108; 2721 Lake, *73–74*; 3001 Lake, *108*–09; 3506 Lake, 73–74, *83*; 3601 Lake, 109; 4000 Lake, *108*
Lake Street Bridge, 103
Lake Street Council, 104
Lake Street Garage, 108
Lake Street light-rail station, 102
Lake Street streetcar line, 69
Lake Street–Marshall Avenue Bridge, *3*, *12–13*, *19*, 82; first Lake Street Bridge, 12–13
Lake Theatre (2721 Lake Street), *73–74*
Lakewood Cemetery, 25
Lansing (MI), 93
Larsen, Andrew, *38*
Latin American, 107
Latinos, 107–08
Laughing Water (in Longfellow's *The Song of Hiawatha*), 66–67
Lauritzen Wagon and Blacksmith Shop (3012 Minnehaha Avenue), 37
Lauritzen, Christian, 37
Lauritzen, Hilleborg, 37
Lewis, Henry, 4, *5*
Lewis, Meriwether, 19
Libby House (3107 28th Avenue), *33*
Libby, Allen, 33–34
Libby, Byron, 33
Libby, Gertrude, 33
Libby, Hannah Garvey, 33–34
Libby, Lewis, 33
Libby, Mabel, 33
Libby, Myrtle, 33
Libby, Viola, 33
Liebenberg and Kaplan, 75
light rail transit (LRT), 105–06
Lincoln, Abraham (Pres.), 20
Little Falls Creek, 4, 66
Lock and Dam No. 1, 3, 9–10, *11*, *13*, 14, 102
Long, Stephen, 5
Longfellow (name), ix
Longfellow Avenue, *22*
Longfellow community (neighborhood), viii, ix–x, 2, 4, 7, 9, 12, 14–15, 18–19, 21–22, 24–25, 30, *31*, 32, *33*, 36, *38*, 39–41, 44–45, 48, 56, 58, 62–63, 69, 72, 74, 78–84, 85–86, 88–89, 95–96, 98, 100,

Longfellow community *continued*
102–04, 107, 109–10, *114*; dairies, 38, 40, 85; "downtown Longfellow" (27th and Lake), 79, 107; grain elevators, 95, 98; housing styles, 85; rain gardens, 110; bungalow, 27, 83

Longfellow Community Council (LCC), ix, 3, 16, 105, 107, 109–11, 113; Neighborhood Revitalization Program, 16; River Gorge Committee, 15–16, 109

Longfellow Field, 35

Longfellow Gardens, *62*, 64, 67–68, 105

Longfellow House, 68

Longfellow Mercantile Company, 92

Longfellow Park, *32*, 35, *81*, 102

Longfellow School, *32*, 33–35, 86, *87*, 88

Longfellow Station, 113

Longfellow, Henry Wadsworth (poet), ix, 20, 66, 68, 88

Longfellow/Seward Greenway section, 104–05

Los Angeles, 27–28

Los Gallos, 108

Louisiana Purchase (1803), 19

Louisville (KY), 93

LRT, 106

Luella A. Anderson Addition, 81, 85

Lutheran Children's Friend Societies (regional organization), 51

Lutheran Children's Friend Society (LCFS; 3624 Edmund Boulevard), 51–52; 3606 West River Road, *51–52*

Lutheran Church-Missouri Synod, 51

Lutheran Social Services (LSS), 51–52

MacFarlane, W. C., 92

Maine, 24, 33

Makoce Wakan (where the Mississippi and Minnesota Rivers join), 19

Mall of America, 106

Mankato, 20, 41

Manny's Tortas, 108

Map of Fort Snelling and Vicinity, *19*

Marshall Avenue (St. Paul), 51

Martin Olav Sabo Midtown Greenway Bridge, *102*

Martin, D. A., 95

Martin, Jake, 35

Martin, Richard, 52

Massachusetts, 68

Mayo Clinic, 55

McMahon's Irish Pub, 109

Mdote (also *Bdote*, juncture of the Mississippi and Minnesota Rivers), 19

Meeker Island, 8–10, 24, 26, *114*

Meeker Island Lock and Dam, *8–9*, 10

Meeker, Bradley B., 10, 26

Merrill, Eufanant 25

Metro Produce, *111*–12

Metro Transit, 13, 82, 103

Metropolitan Drainage Commission of Minneapolis and St. Paul, 14–15

Mexican, 107–08

Michael J. Dowling School for Crippled Children (3900 West River Parkway), *49–50*, 86

Michigan, 93

Midtown Greenway, ix, x, 102, 104–05

Midway district (St. Paul), 63

Midwest, 28

Mill City, 100

Milwaukee, 69

Milwaukee Road (Chicago, Milwaukee, and St. Paul Railway), 95

Milwaukee, St. Paul and Minneapolis Railroad, 89

Minneapolis, ix, 2, 3, *5*, 7–8, 10, 12, 14–15, *18*, 20–22, 27–28, 30, 34, 37, 40, 44, 49, 51–52, 55, 62–64, 72, 75, 79, 83, 88–89, 93, 95, 100, 103, 106, 109, 111; downtown, 72; grain trading and milling, 98; south Minneapolis, ix, 41–42, 58, 69, 72–74, 82, 104; warehouse district, 25

Minneapolis Board of Education, 49, 87–88

Minneapolis Board of Park Commissioners, 67

Minneapolis City Council, 58

Minneapolis Harvester Works, 41, 79, 89

Minneapolis Journal, 58, 65, 70

Minneapolis Labor Review, 75

Minneapolis Library Board, 68

Minneapolis Millers, 65

Minneapolis Milling Company, 98, *98–99*

Minneapolis Park and Recreation Board, 3, 15–16, 68

Minneapolis Planning Department, ix

Minneapolis Public Library, 73

Minneapolis Public Schools, 34–35, 56

Minneapolis Steel and Machinery (MSMC), 30, *78*, 83, *90–92*

Minneapolis Threshing Machine Company, 92

Minneapolis Township, 33

Minneapolis, Lyndale and Minnetonka Motor Line, 64

Minneapolis-Moline Fire Brigade, *93*

Minneapolis-Moline Tractor Company, 21, 79, *91–93*, 94

Minnehaha (in Longfellow's *The Song of Hiawatha*), ix, 66–67

Minnehaha (name for parks, roads, and schools), ix, 20, 66

Minnehaha Academy, 45, *45*

Minnehaha Avenue, x, 2, *18–19*, 21, 27, *30*, *32–34*, *36–37*, *39*, 45–46, 56, *58–59*, 63–64, *65*, 73, 75, *78*, 79, *80*, *81–82*, 83, 86–87, *89*, 92, 94, 102, 107, 109, 113; 2942 Minnehaha, *32;* 3010 Minnehaha, *36–37;* 3012 Minnehaha, 37; 3136 Minnehaha, 37; 3950–3954 Minnehaha, *74–75*

Minnehaha Creek (Brown's Creek), 9, *22*, 68, 105

Minnehaha Dairy, 39

Minnehaha Driving Park, 62–63, *64–65*, 67

Minnehaha Driving Park Association, 63

Minnehaha Elevator, *97–98*

Minnehaha Falls, ix, x, 4, 8, 23, *23*, 62, 66–67

Minnehaha Falls–Fort Snelling streetcar line, 81, *82*

Minnehaha Furniture and Carpet Company, 37

Minnehaha Mall, 88, 113

Minnehaha Park, ix,, 2, 3, 30, 39–40, 64, *66–6*, 68, 81, 105, 113

Minnehaha School, 59

Minnehaha streetcar line, 59

Minnehaha Theater, 73–75

Minnesota, ix, x, 4, 7–8, 10, 15, 18–20, 25, 28, 41, 49, *50*, 51, 62, 66–67, 105; Civil War volunteers, 20, 41; dairy farms, 38

Minnesota Commercial Railroad, 104–05

Minnesota Highway 55, 68, 105; Highway 62, 105

Minnesota Historical Society, 75

Minnesota Legislature, 67

Minnesota Malleable Iron Company, 90

Minnesota Republican, 26

Minnesota River (St. Peter's River), 4, 7, 18–20, 21

Minnesota State Fair, 48, 63

Minnesota State Medical Society, 28

Minnesota Territory, 8, 22, 24, 26–27; Territorial Supreme Court, 10

Minnesota Veterans Home, 39–40

Miss Minneapolis brand, *98*

Mississippi River, ix, x, 2–3, 4, *6*, 7–10, 12–15, 45, 66, 73, 79–84, 103–05, 108–09, 110, *114*; gorge, 5–6, 8, 14–15, 16, 20–22, 24–27, 30, 38–39, 40, 50, 109

Mississippi River Improvement and Manufacturing Company, 26

Mississippi Watershed Management Organization, 110

Missouri River, 19

Moffett mansion, 46

Moline (IL), 93

Moline Implement Company, 92

Molly Quinn's, 108

Monarch 1 and 2 grain elevators, 95

Monarch Elevator Company, *92*, 95

Monroe, John, 48

Montana, 41

Montgomery, Robert, 75

Montreal, 69

Morrill, G. L. (Rev.), 69

Morrison, Dorilus (Mayor), 83, 89

Mosaic of the Americas: Many Strengths, Many Struggles (tile mosaic), *107*

Moulton and Keith, 2, *26*

Moulton, Bell, 25

Moulton, Dorwin E., *24–25*, *26–27*

Moulton, Pamelia Gardner, 25

Mudjekeewis (in Longfellow's *The Song of Hiawatha*), 67

Napa County (CA), 28

National Register of Historic Places, 100

National Tea and National Food Stores (NFS), 58

Native Americans, *18*, 19; stories, x, 66

Nawadaha, ix

Nebraska, 18, 20

Neighborhood Revitalization Program, 105, 110

Nelson Dairy Farm, *39*

Nelson, Martin, *39*–40, 46–47

Nelson, Martinus, 37

Nelson, Victor, 5, 40

New England, x, 18, 24, 44

Niagara Falls, 6

Nicollet Avenue, 64–65

Nicollet County, 41

Nicollet Island, 7

Nicollet Park, 65

Nine Mile Creek, 7

Ninth Ward, 111

No. 7 Metro Transit bus route, 82; No. 21 route, 82; No. 24 route, 82

Nokomis (in Longfellow's *The Song of Hiawatha*), 67; name, ix

Nokomis Theater, 72

NoLo (North Longfellow) Park, 112

Northwest Electronics Institute, 87

Northwestern Tile and Marble, 42

Norway (and Norwegian immigrants), 38, 44–45

Oak Hill Cemetery, 34

Oaks Hiawatha Station, 113

Oddfellows Building (2707 Lake Street), 72, 108

Oh Boy Chicken Shack, 48

Ohio River, 27

Ohio, 23, 44
Ojibwe, ix
Oklahoma (Indian) Territory, 41
Old Territorial Road (Trail), 21
"Olympian," 12
Orpheum Theater, 72
Owahmenah ("falling water," Falls of St. Anthony), 19
O-Wa-Mni ("whirlpool," Falls of St. Anthony), 19

P.S. Wish You Were Here (sculpture), 113
Panic of 1857, 18, 24–26
Panic of 1893, 30, 33, 38, 81, 83
Patrick's Cabaret, 37
Pence Opera House, 72
Perkins, Charles E., 59, 84
Petersen, Hjalmar (Gov.), *50*
Pettijohn, Eli, 4
Pig's Eye Island, 3
Pig's Eye sewage treatment plant, 15
Pike Island, 19–20
Pike, Zebulon, 4, 19
Platteville limestone, 6
Pond, Samuel, 19
Poodle Club (3001 Lake Street), *108*–09
Popeye's (3601 East Lake), 109
Pre-emption Act (1855), 22
Princess Depot, 68
Progressive Era, 49
Purina Chow, 99
Purina Mills, *100*, *106*, 113
Quebec, 69
Quigley family, 97
Quigley, Allen, 97–98
Quigley, James, 97

R & R Hall, 59
Radio Rey, 107
Rainbow Foods, 58, 108
Ralston Purina, 99
Ramsey (MN), 3
Rasmussen dairy farm, *40*
Rasmussen, Rasmus, *40*
Record, James L., 90–91
Red Owl, 58
Reid, James, 41
Relf, Annette (Sister), 53
Remington, Frederic, ix
Resource Center of the Americas, *107*
Rialto Theater, 72
River Gorge Stewards, 16
River Warren, 6
Riverview Theater (3800 42nd Avenue), *63*, 75–76

Robbinsdale, 75
Robinson, Bessie, 35, *35*
Roosevelt, Franklin D. (Pres.) and Eleanor, *50; 97*
Roosevelt, Theodore (Pres.), 92
Rosebud Theater, 72
Round Table Club, 44
Rustad Grocery (3301 31st Avenue), *56*–57
Rustad, Arne, *57*
Rustad, Emmet, *57*

Sabbath, 65
Sabo, Martin (Cong.), 105
St. Anthony, 18, 20, 22, 25–27, 98
St. Barnabas (Polio) Hospital, 55
St. James African Methodist Episcopal (AME) Church (3600 Snelling Avenue), 48
St. James Hotel, 25
St. Louis Park, 95
St. Paul, 3, 6–7, *9*, *12*–13, *14*–15, 20–22, 26, 41, 63, 82, 89, 105, 108
St. Peter sandstone, 6
St. Peter's (Minnesota) River, 4
Sancho (Newfoundland dog), 24
Sandstone (MN), 51
Sanford Junior High, 86, *88*
Sanford, Maria Louise (Prof.), 88
Sauna 27, 107
Savage, Marion, *64*
Scandinavia (and Scandinavian immigrants), *38*, *39*, 44–45, 47
Schiff, Gary, 111
School District 108, 33–34
Schoolcraft, Henry Rowe, 66
Scott, Henry B., 59, 84
Scully, Patrick, 37
Sears, Roebuck, and Company, 85
Second Empire style, 34
Seierson house (2801 31st Avenue), *38*
Seierson, Mads, *38*
Selby-Lake interurban streetcar line, 12, *78*, 82, *83*
Seven Oaks Bakery (3149 38th Avenue), *60*
Seven Oaks Corporation, ix, 59, 84; name, 84; subdivisions, 59–60, *84*
Seven Oaks Improvement Association, 58–60; district, *60*
Seward Neighborhood Group, 110
Seward neighborhood, ix, 24, 26, 28, 104, 110
Sheltering Arms Orphanage, 40, 44, 52–53, 54–56
Shooting the Chutes, 69, *70*–*71*
Short Line railroad bridge, *2*, *3*, *7*, 9–*10*, 12, 26, 105

Shubert Theatre, 72
Simmons School, 86–87
Simmons, Henry, 87
Sister Kenny, 55
Smith, Mrs. C. A., 4
Snelling (name), 21
Snelling Avenue, 21, 37, 45, *48*, 113; 3600 Snelling, 48; 3624 Snelling, 48; 3633 Snelling, 48
Snelling, Josiah (Col.), *21*
Snelling,, Abigail, 21
Social Security, 47, 54
Sommerfest, 47
Song of Hiawatha (poem by Henry Wadsworth Longfellow), ix, 20, 66, 88
Sorenson, Robert James, *46*
South Dakota, 18, 20
South Minneapolis addition, 89
South (region of U.S.), the, 48
Southtown, ix
Southwest LRT trail, 105
Spanish language, 107–08
Stanley, James, 85
State of Minnesota, 54
Stebbins, Edward Somerby, 87
Stevens, John, 4, *18*, 20
Stowe School, 86, 88
Stowe, Harriet Beecher, 88
Summit Avenue (St. Paul), 12
Sunfed Flour, 98
Sweden (and Swedish immigrants), 38, 44–45

Taliaferro, Lawrence, 19
Target, 88, 113
Thai, 108
Thatcher, Bill, 97
Thoreau, Henry David, 67
Tiro Industries, 111
Toro, 91
Traverse des Sioux treaty (1851), 18, 20–21
Trinity Apartments, 113
Tuttle, Mary, 23
Twain, Mark (Samuel L. Clemens), 67
Twin Cities, 3, 14, 20, 46–48, 51, 62–63, 69, *91*
Twin City Iron Works, 90
Twin City Rapid Transit Company (TCRT), 12, 81

Unci Maka ("Grandmother Earth," earth), 19
Unitarian Church, 87
United States (U.S.), 12, 22, 37, 41, 55, 72, 81, 91; Army, 66; Army Corps of Engineers (the Corps), 7–10; history, 20, 26; troops, 20; War Department, 22

University of Minnesota, 8, 41, 56, 88
Upper Midwest, ix, 64
Urban Environmental Learning Center, 50

Vanatta, Julia, *110*
Vanderburgh Presbyterian Church, 70
Vermont, 24
Victory Christian Center, 74
Virginia (steamboat), 66
Volk, Sidney and William, 75

Walter A. Wood Harvester Company, 84–85, 89
Walton, Edmund, 59–60
Walton's Fifth Division, 84
Walton's Home Builder, *84*, 85
War of 1812, 21
Washburn Crosby Company, 98
Washington Avenue, 25
Washington, D.C., 21
Wass Addition, 28
Wass, Anness, 23, 27–28
Wass, John and Eliza, 27–28
Wass, Lizzie, 23, 27–28

Watershed Friendly Yard Tour, *110*, 111
Waubun Picnic Area, 68
West River Commons, *102*, 112, *113*
West River Parkway, 19, 40, 47, 50, *47*, *51*–*53*, 56, 85, *102*, 104–05, 112–13, *113*; 3030–3034 West River, *47*; 3606 West River, *51*–*52*; 3900 West River, 49–50, 86; bike path, 102
Whipple, Henry B. (Episcopal Bishop), 20
White City (Chicago), 69
White Motor Company, 93
Williams, Sylestus Phelps, 48
Winchell Trail, 8, 19
Winchell, Newton Horace, 8, *8*
Wisconsin, 25
Women's Co-Operative Alliance, 42, 57, 59, 73–74
Women's Medical College of Chicago, 27, 28
Wonderland Fairy Theater, 69
Wonderland Limited, *71*
Wonderland Park, *62*, 69–70, 72, 82, 103
Wonderland Park Milwaukee, 69
Works Progress Administration (WPA), 8, 50, 68
World War I, 48–49, 91, 98
World War II, x, 7, 10, 14, 36–37, 48, 54, 57, 81, 84–85, 87, 93, 97
Wright, Frank Lloyd, 85

Xcel Energy, 10